TRAVEL THE WORLD –
FOR FREE

Jack Freemont

Table Of Contents

COPYRIGHT

INTRODUCTION

"Travel writing is not only the most glamorous job in the world - it's also the most fun - and it is easy to do!"

So says Jack Freemont (a pen name - more on that in a moment), world-renowned travel writer and photographer.

You'll have seen his videos on international TV, probably read his words online and in the newspapers - and now he not only shows you how easy it is for you to travel the world and stay in comfort for free, he also "spills the beans" with the contents of his contacts book.

He shows you how to immediately get legitimate access to the secret twice monthly PDF bulletin which lists the latest hotels, reports, airlines, even whole countries, all of whom want to pay for everything to get you to visit them!

He also supplies the full details of where to place your pictures or story - so you often get famous, too!

He lists places desperate for your reports (paying at least a dollar a word!) and / or pictures (paying $30 each - and upwards).

Yes, TV stations, newspapers and websites want your travel experiences AND they want your pictures!

You don't need some really expensive camera - almost all of your pictures ("pix" in the jargon) will be published online, so even your camera phone is perfect!

In this fun to read, yet fact-packed edition, Jack takes you be the hand and shows you not only how easy it is to get to visit the greatest hotels, theme parks, cruise lines, resorts and spas in the world - but also how to get there for free by air - often in First Class.

Why would these places want to do this?

Every country, every hotel, every airline has a massive marketing budget - budgets that are actually increased in times of recession.

Advertising costs a fortune, especially on a national or international basis.

But if you have a simple blog, can write a little about your experience, perhaps add a few pictures, you'll never pay to stay and travel again.

Now, this bit is important.

You do not need to be some fluent, fully trained writer.

You write about what you see, what you do, in normal everyday words.

This is because the resorts etc want "honest, everyday language" - as the public will trust it more - certainly more than any paid TV or Press advertising campaign.

There's another reason, too.

You will add a link to the hotel, resort, airline etc in your writing - which counts as a "backlink" to the site - it's a sort of vote, which Google and the other search engines love.

This moves the place you stay with / the company you travel with higher up the listings on Google - which is good for them - and your real opinion is much more trusted than any advertising or travel website!

Remember, you taking an extra seat (or two - take your partner / family in almost all cases) on an aircraft, a room in a hotel or a cabin on a cruise liner costs almost nothing to the supplier - but your comments are like gold dust to them!

Now, we'll let you into a little extra secret.

Jack Freemont is not his real name - he would be ostracized by the other Travel Writers who sail and fly around the world for free if they know who he was!

They love their lifestyles and their secrets - and now you can, too.

But "Jack" really reveals all - all the extras you can obtain (everything from free top of the range luggage to warm clothes (or swimsuits and sunglasses!) as these companies want publicity for their products too!). These are revealed in the top secret twice-monthly, free, newsletter.

As well as listing the people / departments to contact (emails / names / phone numbers as appropriate), he gives you full access to some private websites which list special "Press Trips".

These offer you the chance to travel with other website owners and get lots of extra - as well as travel from your local airport, the host meets you at the destination airport (in some countries, they meet you on board the aircraft after it lands - you are sat at the front, so that you can be priority disembarked and whisked, in a minibus or limo from the aircraft steps, through the VIP security section and straight to the resort.

Your bags mysteriously appear in your room before you do (they're priority disembarked, too!).

Your tickets are marked with a special three letter code (not VIP, in case you were wondering - more important than that!) which ensures that all the airline staff treat you to the best of everything.

At the resort / hotel/ cruise ship, you are whisked straight to the best facilities - no credit card deposits, nothing to pay for - everything is "comped" (jargon for "made complimentary").

Often, your local airport will "comp" your parking whilst you're away - they want to make a good impression, too!

So, whether you want just to travel on your annual holiday with your family or you want to do as Jack does and explore the planet for one or two weeks every month, get his book right now - you could be travelling next week!

TRAVEL FOR FREE

"The most fun you can have with your clothes on" is a bit of a cliche, but my exploits around our planet over the last 20 years do justify the phrase.

Here's just some of the exciting things I've recently done - all for free - and there's no reason why you can't do the same.

MOROCCO

On a trip to Morocco with a new airline, I was given the front row of the aircraft to myself.

And when I say the whole row, I mean BOTH sides of the aisle!

This was done to ensure I had complete privacy, whilst the airline's top stewards really looked after me with the best food wines and entertainment.

After we landed, I was made buy a delightful lady from the Moroccan tourist board.

She came on board the aircraft, the crew having kept the "class-divider" curtains behind me closed.

She took me down the steps of the aircraft, just the 2 of us, and onto a waiting minibus.

We drove all of 30 yards to the VIP security, where she handed my passport to a very smartly dressed border guard, who saluted me!

He said, with a genuinely welcoming smile 'Welcome to Morocco, Sir!'

So now we went back to the same minibus and onto my five-star hotel. I suddenly asked 'what about my luggage?'

My new friend merely smiled and said "already on board Sir!".

To this day, I don't know how they did it, but somehow my bags were marked at my departure airport "express" or "CIP" and loaded into the minibus before the steps had even reached the aircraft.

That's the sort of service I've now become used to!

(Aside: "CIP. Thought you'd never ask! You've probably heard of VIP, "very important person", yes?

CIP is far more important. This stands for "commercially important person" and is also often seen on your tickets when you're travelling as a travel writer.

This is so the check-in staff can upgrade you to the lounges etc and is also emphasised on the passenger lists. The aircraft crew, including the pilots, get these for each flight.

This system means everyone knows that you are commercially important to the airline).

As you can imagine, this make sure you are always exceptionally well looked after!

I could talk for pages about the country of Morocco, one of my favorites, and how welcoming everybody is.

However that's not the purpose of the book as I want you to explore this and every other country for yourself - but it's a good example of a country that isn't why any means wealthy, but which relies on people like you and I writing about them and encouraging other visitors.

EGYPT

I regularly visit another favorite country Egypt, at the repeated invitations of their tourist board.

One of the things I always like to do, much to the amusement of my local guide (on nearly all of these visits a guide will escort you anywhere and everywhere you want, take you to the fronts of queues at museums, arrange for you to be checked in hotels automatically, no queueing for taxes, no waiting for anything at any time) is just sit and watch the traffic in Cairo, Egypt's capital.

I have been lucky enough to have done the pyramids at Giza three times now, but on my most recent visit, I was taken inside the great Pyramid, deep inside where the tombs were originally held.

One of my favorite museums is the Cairo Museum but this always has long queues.

I've never queued, of course - the armed guards smartly salute me and my guide on every visit and I'm taken straight through, usually not having to even pass through the security and the metal detectors!

If you go to the Cairo Museum as a normal tourist, the only place to eat and drink is a frankly rather scruffy cafe (albeit a very cheap one!) to the front and middle of the Museum.

However if you're there is a VIP guest, a travel writer, you are taken into the private staff restaurant at the back with the food and drink is, frankly astonishing (and free, of course!).

I tend not to do cruises on the Nile - it's just not my thing - but the tourist board will always supply you a small plane to fly you down to the southern cities and see places like the Valley of the Kings or Karnak.

The planes are sometimes a bit like something out of an Indiana Jones movie - but at least you get to sit, often with the pilot.

And, yes I have taken a (very short) go at the controls, whilst following the Nile.

Wonderful. And money couldn't buy this!

I never tire of visiting this area, and have become quite an (unintentional!) expert on hieroglyphics and Egyptian history!

JORDAN

I recently spent Christmas in Jordan, a place like not thought of previously visiting, and I had a terrific time.

Again, I was met at the airport (part of which incidentally is actually in Israel!)

My partner and I were whisked in an executive minibus to the town of Petra where we were checked in to (only) a 3 star hotel, but it was still the best in town!

Not only would we get the full "Petra, the Rose Red City, as old as time iteself" tour, at our own pace the next day, but we were also supplied with a donkey and cart to save the long walk down the siq into the Treasury area of Petra.

We were told that we would be visiting again that evening, which surprised me as I knew that the siq is closed on a night as it normally has no lighting etc.

What they did for me and a few other people, perhaps 20 others in total (the others had paid over $120 each for the three-hour tour) was to put sand and candles into brown paper bags for the 3 mile walk, thus lighting our way into the area outside the Treasury building - which itself had a few candles.

Musicians mysteriously played and appeared all around us in a truly magical, romantic evening.

After a night-time tour were escorted back out again in a private luxury minibus - while the others, who paid all the money, were queueing up for their coaches.

I also toured the capital, Amman, and was allowed into the (closed at the time) museum where the original Dead Sea Scrolls are on display.

I also stood where Pope John Paul stood, overlooking Jerusalem, Bethlehem and the Holy land.

The local priest also escorted me around the specially built church, which was officially opened by the Pope on his visit.

BELGIUM

A country I usually describe as "the unknown country' is Belgium, a place I visit at least once a year.

My heart always lifts as I go into the main square and see what excitement they have for me this time!

For example every 4 years the whole square is filled with around 7 million flowers, making vastly intricate patterns on the cobbles.

Remember the buildings around you here are, at their newest, some 400 to 500 years old.

Now, I'm not much of a drinker, but the bars, the amount of beer, the sheer range of beers which are available in Belgium is astonishing.

Fortunately they are also famous for their chocolate, which I love, and for their lace, which I am always given fantastic samples of – and these make great presents for friends and family when I return.

Last time I stayed at the new Charles Forte hotel was given the second-best suite (the top suites are over $1000 a night and not really what I required!)

All food, wine, everything, was of course freely available to me.

I must say I gave the hotel a great review as everywhere everyone there went out of their way to make me very comfortable.

It's worth pointing out to you, again, that whilst *every* guest in a hotel is important to them, someone who has the facility to publish, to write, to broadcast, to talk about their visit, is considered even more important as hotels and suchlike have such massive advertising budgets ... but we as the public, tend to prefer and trust more in the words of our fellow man, than we do some glossy advert.

And long may that situation last!

SWITZERLAND

I never tire of visiting Switzerland, both in summer and winter.

Indeed, to go to the same area in both the seasons and see just how different they are never seizes to please me.

One of my favorite trips is a railway train up inside a mountain.

Yes! There is a train to the top of the Jungfrau Mountain which goes up inside the Eiger and then stops on its' way through the mountains and ends at the highest railway station in all of Europe!

What's great is that the train stops twice on the way up you get off and walk along a narrow corridor carved out of solid rock and see a huge window.
You are then looking out onto the North face of the Eiger - with mountaineers climbing past you!

I often describe my working life as quite surreal, but being dressed quite normally and looking out at Mountaineers climbing such a mighty mountain is very strange...

At the top of the Jungfrau mountain, when you get off the train, is an ice tunnel where all the items are carved from solid ice ... but tend not to melt - you are, after all, thousands of feet up a mountain!

As you travel the world you will find that the best hotel managers tend to be Swiss, they seem to really understand what guests want, they tend to be multilingual, and they really want to make you have an excellent stay at the hotel.

This means that the hotels in Switzerland, which are always manned and staffed by native Swiss, tend to be amongst the best in the world of course.

CRUISES

It's not all hotels of course!

I've done a few cruises, and although they're not really "me", I do find them a relaxing way of seeing lots of countries in one or 2 weeks.

My favorites are those around the Mediterranean where you can visit France, Spain, Italy (including Pompeii and Sicily), Tunisia and Corsica for example.

NORWAY

Last year I was invited to an island off the coast of Norway.

The timings of the flights, however, made it very difficult, so the tourist board actually arrange for me to have a helicopter to do the last 60 miles.

Now, I love helicopters, but have always found them very expensive!

This flight, of course, was free – moreover, the pilot not only gave me headphones to listen into air traffic control (which is always in English, of course!) but, as were over the North Sea, allowed me to spend a few minutes flying the helicopter.

Now, I did try and do a hover which I'm told is the hardest thing to do in a helicopter - and I can now confirm that I couldn't do that ... indeed the pilot went quite pale at one stage!

Because the area was quite cold I was supplied free of charge clothing, boots, jacket, hat, etc, and these of course I got to keep.

THE AMERICAS

Of course, I appreciate that many of the readers of this book will be based in the United States and will want to travel either within the states or up to Canada or down to parts of South America.

The United States public spends more money on travel writers than any other country in the world, and rightly so, and again I show you later how to contact the various states, the various attractions, as well as the hotel groups cruise companies and so on.

And you really should ask a trip on one of the great trains right across this mighty country.

Also, Canada always welcomes visitors and you really should ensure that you get a trip on one of the trains right across the country. To the south of the United States, most people want to make the excursion of a lifetime to, for example, the Galapagos Islands, aswell as the many other places to visit.

I'm a particular fan of Peru, partly because again the tourist board is so welcoming, but even places like Brazil and Uruguay will welcome you with open arms.

AUSTRALIA / NEW ZEALAND

I realize that I've not mentioned some more my favorite countries, Australia and New Zealand - my apologies for that!

Australia is truly an amazing country, with some of the most welcoming people it is possible to find.

The climate, the roads, the food and the standards of the hotels are all world-class and beyond and again my heart always lifts, when I see the fabulous Sydney Harbor Bridge.

I've been invited to do the walk over the top of that and I must admit I will probably do that on my next visit there.

New Zealand seems to me to be quite beautiful, full of sheep it has to be said, and again the people are very nice but one visit was enough for me.

That's the great thing about this job, of course - you can go back as often as you want or try something once and not worry about any expense!

If you love it / like it, go back time and again, as there's always new places to explore, new hotels opening, new beaches having new facilities, or just new museums which want you to come and report on the contents.

RUSSIA

In the coming year, I am spending more time travelling around the Russian Federation - this is partly because I had my first visit there last year and really enjoyed the place and, secondly, because my (now) partner is from there!

We actually met in Russia, of course, and she now travels the world with me.

Russia is that rare exception when travelling as so few people speak English, whereas in the rest of the world a reasonable knowledge of English will get you by almost anywhere!

I'm therefore very lucky that the Russian tourist board is more than happy to fly and take me by train around this vast nation, and having my own personal translator by my side makes life very easy for both of us!

At the time of writing this part of the book I have a meeting arranged next week with Russian Railways, who want me to do the whole of the trans-Siberian express from Moscow to Vladivostok with a side trip to Mongolia.

As you can imagine I am very excited by this - to me 7 days on a train in total is actually great.

OTHER ADVENTURES / HOLIDAYS

Similarly spa hotels around the world are a fantastic way to just chill for the week.

I'm certainly no sportsman, nor particularly active, but a nice week in a spa hotel with a few visits to the sauna and relaxing in a pool (and I'll admit it, I can't swim!) is rather nice....

All this makes for a great lifestyle – and, as you can imagine, I have no problem choosing girlfriends to come with me!

I should mention here that it's not all travel.

Although I like to explore towns and cities resorts and so on, I am just as happy lounging around a resort hotel or a golf hotel.

Indeed, golf hotels are some of the most welcoming as golf itself is so competitive and hotels with golf courses costs a lot of money to maintain and keep to high standards so they're particularly welcoming to people who can write about them.

I'm not a golfer myself, however but that doesn't stop me taking advantage of these resort style hotels which often have areas for the family, so that usually the man can go off and play golf and the partner and family can go off and, shall we say, enjoy themselves!

I also don't tend to worry too much about making notes whilst I'm 'in resort', as it's called as you always get what is called a press pack during the course of your visit.

I should say that you actually get loads, everything from free books from the museums that you visit to USB sticks, DVDs and so on showing film footage and notes on the area - and this of course cuts down on the amount of work you have to do once you get home!

The facts, figures and details are all there for you!

You need to know that with the invites I get, several each day, I have to turn down over 99% of the invites that I get.

This is irritating at first, but frankly you soon become quite blasé about it!

Indeed the tourist boards often respect you more when you drop a polite note saying that "on this occasion you are busy" doing whatever else and that marks you down as a good travel writer, one who is very much "in demand" and they tend to invite you to more places ... hint!

PUBLIC RELATIONS COMPANIES

This will be a good point to tell you about public relations companies.

Public relations companies will be your new best friend as their job is to charge countries, resorts, airlines etc rather large fees to act as a go-between between the country and travel writers.

Most public relations companies are staffed by young girls who whilst being awfully pleasant tend not to be, on the whole, very bright and indeed often haven't travelled very far.

Don't be put off by this, but don't assume just because you're speaking to some person who have doesn't even understand the country or know where things are - their job is basically to put together you and the country and they charge some quite vast fees, often tens of thousands of pounds per month for doing exactly that.

I've listed some of the PR companies that you will be dealing with along with lists of the countries that they currently deal with.

Do remember that countries / companies change PR companies, often on an annual basis, and this information can change regularly.

However these companies always proudly show on their websites the country's resorts and so on that they deal with along with the name of the person who handles that particular place.

Don't be afraid to send e-mails to these people - and you will be astonished at the amount of stuff you'll get through the post and e-mail and the sheer number of invites that you will get.

Their whole business is built around knowing travel writers, of course - the more "contacts" they have, the more they can charge the country / cruise / hotel etc client!

ORGANIZATIONS TO JOIN

One organization that I want you to join straightaway, today, is the international Travel Writers Alliance, which is worldwide but based in London.

They issue a 40 or 50 page PDF every 2 weeks and this lists the very latest offer's available to you - far too many, all for free, to even consider covering all of them!

I occasionally show friends part of this document and they are totally astonished at the range and depth of opportunities available to me!

This not only lists PR companies and ongoing invites - for example, hotels, resorts airlines, travel companies and so on to whom you are welcome to contact at any time (therefore contact details are in every issue), but also private invites to special events, perhaps a theatre, a new museum in some exotic part of the world, or just a fact-finding trip to some glamorous city or resort.

Although the existence of the Alliance is kept secret, by using the details below you can join immediately, and will be sent the secret PDF every 2 weeks - and will also have access to lots of extra information which is held on their website.

Here's the details:

To register with the International Travel Writers Alliance visit:

http://www.itwalliance.com

Click to enter the site and click on "Register as a member".

Another membership (free to you – the fees are paid by the holiday companies!) site to join is

http://www.TravelWriters.com

Here are some references from users of this great site:

"I just got back from a fabulous trip to Thailand as a result of one of your listings. In addition to the story assignment that qualified me for this trip, I have gleaned months of story material that I will now savor and share with many new markets. This has opened a door to amazing opportunities for me."

Craig Pulsifer, Writer & Photographer

Your mailings and your website offerings are soooo helpful and supportive. I just got back from writers' trip to Alaska, thanks to your notice. Needless to say, the trip was outstanding, and Alaska will get many great stories from me as a result.
Keep up the GREAT WORK!

Naomi K. Shapiro, Independent writer

A short note from a professional travel journalist and photographer based in London. I've subscribed to the service, and it's invaluable. I just want to extend my thanks for the press trips and press releases and information distributed. Keep up the excellent work,

kind thoughts, Yemi Maye.

Just wanted to say I think you are doing a great job. I just came off a press trip and gave your address to several other writers.

Thanks, sue lynn

The site correctly describes itself as "a professional network of travel writers, editors and members of the public relations community.

Travelwriters.com is based on a simple principle: to connect top-tier writers with editors, PR agencies, tourism professionals, CVBs and tour operators, nurturing the important link that so heavily influences the travel media".

Membership is free and they post a lot of press trips, particularly for the American market.

http://www.travelwriters.com/presstrips/view/listview.asp

Even more useful, however, is their bulletin board, where thousands of travel writers gather to discuss ideas, opportunities - and find good contacts.

If you're looking to stay at a particular resort or need a contact at a specific airline, this is the place to ask.

Also see:

http://www.travelwriters.com/pressreleases/view/listview.asp

Which has a great list of press releases, which are often very useful - do look here at least weekly, please!

http://www.mediakitty.com/Default.aspx

Use Media Kitty to find:

- experts, sources and leads

- news and story ideas

- media trip invitations

- jobs and assignments

- contacts worldwide

Over 9,000 members currently - very helpful staff and very good press trips and contacts.

Journalists and sources need to connect and Media Kitty makes that easy.

Here's how:

Travel writers post requests for story assistance

PR people and businesses post news releases and offers for journalists to experience their products and services

Each contributes what they can to the "kitty" and each takes something away.

What's more, Media Kitty has an online directory of journalism and PR sources. Post links to your website, blog, newsroom, image bank or Twitterfeed.

There's space for your picture, contact details, special interests and other relevant details. Save contacts and postings of interest to "My Kitty" – your online file drawer.

http://www.thetravelwriterslife.com/category/sell-stories/

Is a wonderful site where I get many of my best hints and ideas for when I actually want to sell my stories.

Other groups which will supply you with loads of places to visit for free, as well as ideas for stories and photo's include:

http://www.thetravelwriterslife.com/category/sell-stories/

Is a wonderful site where I get many of my best hints and ideas for when I actually want to sell my stories.

Other groups which will supply you with loads of places to visit for free, as well as ideas for stories and photo's include:

International Food, Wine & Travel Writers Association.

A global network of people involved in the hospitality and lifestyle fields - and the people who promote them by informing others about them.

A non-profit organization, run by and for the benefit of members, and has been since it was founded in Paris in 1954.

American Society of Journalists and Authors.

Helps professional freelance writers advance their writing careers.

North American Travel Journalists.

The "premier professional association of writers, photographers, editors, and tourism professionals dedicated to redefining professional development for the travel industry."

Society of American Travel Writers.

Now in its 50th year, SATW promotes responsible journalism, supports and develops members, and encourages conservation and preservation of travel resources worldwide.

Travel Media Association of Canada.

"A handful of visionary, Toronto-based travel journalists founded the Travel Media Association of Canada (TMAC) in 1994.

They saw the need to bring the country's travel media and tourism industry closer together — in effect, the founders struck a professional relationship between the two groups by creating TMAC."

http://www.travelmedia.ca/

British Guild of Travel Writers.

"Founded in 1960, the British Guild of Travel Writers is an association of over 270 writers, editors, photographers, producers, radio and television presenters involved in the world of travel."

http://www.bgtw.org/

Outdoor Writers' Guild (UK).

Founded in 1980 by a group of like-minded writers with a direct interest in equipment and clothing for the outdoors.

Members includes writers, authors, photographers, designers, journalists, artists, illustrators, editors, broadcasters, copywriters, content-providers, lecturers, public speakers, and consultants.

http://www.owpg.org.uk/

Australian Society of Travel Writers.

Celebrated its 30th year in 2006! A non-profit organization, "dedicated to reporting on the travel industry and serving the interests of the traveling public, promoting international understanding and good will, and promoting unbiased reporting of information on travel topics."

National Association of Woman Writers.

Founded in 2001, they have over 3000 members worldwide. NAWW connects and educates members through books, CDs, tele-events, physical chapter events and much more.

A weekly newsletter goes out to over 3,000 women writers, editors, and publishers!

Midwest Travel Writers Association. Is an organization of travel professionals, including writers, photographers, and travel publicists.

"Since we all live in one of the 13 Midwestern states (Illinois, Indiana, Iowa, Kansas, Kentucky, Michigan, Minnesota, Missouri,

Nebraska, North Dakota, Ohio, South Dakota and Wisconsin), we're experts in the wide variety of travel opportunities these states offer."

WEB SITES

You can travel the world for free and put your reports on your own website.

An easy, free, way to start is by going to blogger.com, which is owned by Google.

There are full details on how to easily and quickly do this here:

http://www.blogger.com

Not only is this a really easy way to add your words and pictures to a website, but you'll find that Google lists your details within a few hours.

This means that you can send links both to your site and to Google, where editors, publishers and travel companies can see your posts – and offer you more work and more free travel!

These sites, below, are all produced by people just like you, people who decide to travel for free, and who have made a great success of it.

Do have a good read of each, please – and keep an eye on what they do, where they go, what they write and photograph.

1. Down The Road
www.downtheroad.org
Quote: "We are Tim and Cindie Travis, an ordinary American couple who decided to live out our dreams. We saved our money, quit our jobs, sold our possessions, and set off to travel around the world by bicycle. We left our home in Arizona, USA on March 31, 2002 and have been on the road ever since. Our plan is to continue to bicycle tour and travel for the next several years."

2. Gone Walkabout
www.gonewalkabout.com
Quote: "The term Walkabout comes from the Australian Aboriginal. The idea is that a person can get so caught up in one's work, obligations and duties that the truly important parts of one's self become lost. From there it is a downward spiral as one gets farther and farther from the true self. A crisis situation usually develops that awakens the wayward to the absent true self.

It is at this time that one must go on walkabout. All possessions are left behind (except for essential items) and one starts walking.

Metaphorically speaking, the journey goes on until you meet yourself. Once you find yourself, you sit down and have a long talk about what one has learned, felt and done in each other's absence. One talks until there is nothing left to say — the truly important things cannot be said. If one is lucky, after everything has been said and unsaid, one looks up and sees only one person instead of the previous two."

3. Modern Gonzo

www.moderngonzo.com
Quote: "My tiny Modern Gonzo has now become a horde of inspiration from my journeys to over 50 countries (and counting) on 6 continents. I built and maintain the site myself, for I'm certain that within its pages lies a spark that can help others fire up their dreams too. Things appear to happen for a reason after all. You hear about these dream stories, and then one day, you wake up and find yourself living one. "

4. Expedition 360
www.expedition360.com
Quote: "I had absolutely no interest in the watery sections of such a proposal, having always failed to be convinced by recreational mariners of the supposed fun to be derived from being cold, wet and seasick all at the same time and for extended periods of time.
But the overland sections sounded intriguing: my head was filled with wildly romantic images of riding bicycles across the steppes of central Asia, trekking through the frozen wilderness of

the Himalayas, staring into the flames of a roaring campfire after a hard day hacking our way through the Amazon jungle.

And the 2 years the expedition was projected to take traveling through predominantly warmer climes sounded like a welcome escape from that cold, wet island known to us natives as England."

5. Let Me Stay For A Day
www.letmestayforaday.com
Quote: "My name is Ramon Stoppelenburg . When I was 24 I left my house in The Netherlands, on May 1, 2001, with a backpack filled with clothing, a digital camera, a laptop, and a mobile phone.

From May 2001 to July 2003 I traveled the world without any money, visiting people who invited me over through this website. I crossed distance with my thumb or with help of sponsors and supporters. In return for all support I wrote about this all in my daily reports on this website."

6. Mark Moxon
www.moxon.net
Quote: "In early 1995 I visited a friend who had just bought a new house. I remember it quite

clearly: at the top of the stairs he had a perfectly formed bathroom in which I had what can only be described as a religious experience. The bathroom was one hundred per cent peach. It had a peach-coloured bath, a peach toilet, peach tiles on the wall and a peach basin on which sat a bar of peach-scented soap.

Hanging on the racks were fluffy peach hand towels that neatly matched the peach carpet below, and sitting on the windowsill was a bowl full of peach-coloured potpourri. I realised then and there that if I didn't do something pretty radical, I was going to end up with a peach bathroom all of my own, and the thought filled me with dread."

7. Where The Hell Is Matt?
www.wherethehellismatt.com
Quote: "Matt is a 29-year-old deadbeat from Connecticut who used to think that all he ever wanted to do in life was make and play videogames. He achieved this goal pretty early and enjoyed it for a while, but eventually realized there might be other stuff he was missing out on. In February of 2003, he quit his job in Brisbane, Australia and used the money he'd saved to wander around the planet until it ran out.

A few months into his trip, a travel buddy gave Matt the idea of dancing everywhere he went and recording it on his camera. This turned out to be a very good idea. Now Matt is quasi-famous as "That guy who dances on the internet. No, not that guy. The other one. No, not him either. I'll send you the link. It's funny."

8. Hitch50

www.hitch50.com

Quote: "Why are we doing this? We both just graduated college and didn't exactly pursue the typical business jobs our classmates were chasing, so we needed something to do. Something fun to do, which involved traveling and meeting people and sharing experiences with them. So... we decided to hitchhike to every state capital, in 50 days or less. This gives us the opportunity to meet fun people and see fun places all over the USA.

As much as we're into seeing all the great places we'll visit, we're even more excited to meet the people that will take us to those places. Hitch50 isn't really a project about places; it's about people. Are you one of those people?"

9. Vagabonding

www.vagabonding.com

Quote: "I view travel as life's great educator. There's no better way to learn about people and nature and your place in the world.

I got hooked on travel during my final semester in college, when I studied literature and theater in London. After school ended, I stayed in Europe for a year, working at pubs, record stores, and Italian restaurants to fund further travel. I managed to get as far south as Morocco and as far east as Turkey.

Those dramatic, vivid destinations fueled my appetite for more travel, more experiences, further-flung places. The more you travel, the more you realize how little you've seen.

I came home from Europe penniless and began to write for a newspaper in my hometown.

These vagabonding dreams were born at that newspaper. I figured I'd travel around the world and write a column for the paper as I went. Of course, travel is hard to fund on a bottom-rung journalist's salary.

I took a job in Chicago a little later, writing copy for web sites. I'd never seen a web page, had never sent an email before that job. It doesn't seem like a day's gone past since I haven't. I bought the vagabonding.com URL while at that job. That was 1998."

10. The Travel Junkie
www.thetraveljunkie.ca
Quote: "My year around-the-world taught me a lot of things: never turn down an invitation, bargain hard and always carry a roll of toilet paper. Most of all, travelling made me globally aware.

I learned about abducted child soldiers in Northern Uganda; the loss of indigenous culture in Tanzania; the construction of the "separation wall," also dubbed the "apartheid wall," across the disputed Israeli-Palestinian land. I learned that the Turkish government has been accused of denying the Armenian genocide; that despite the AIDS epidemic in Africa, humanitarian aid money often doesn't reach the people it is supposed to help. I learned about the persecution of the Falun Gong and saw the aftermath of the Rwandan genocide.

I may be a McGill University graduate but travel has been the ultimate education. My trip has given me a deeper understanding of what's going on in the world and where I fit within it."

11. The Argonauts

www.theargonauts.com

Quote: "Ask yourself this question, "If you could do anything — anything in the world — what would you do?" You can guess my answer. I feel that life is a gift and that I have only one chance to live. In the words of Henry David Thoreau, "I went to the woods because I wished to live deliberately, to front only the essential facts of life, and see if I could not learn what it had to teach, and not, when I came to die, discover that I had not lived."

And, to be honest, I had more than my fair share of angst and riding around the world was the only option I could see to overcome my malaise and become (or is that prove) to the world who I thought I "should" be."

12. Goliath Expedition

goliath.mail2web.com

Quote: "Many years ago, when based with the Army in Dover, I would stand on the white cliffs looking out across the English Channel at the distant shores of France in wonder.

I swear, some days I could almost see a ragged figure looking back at me, a spectre from my future. I could not help but wonder what he had seen along the way and who he was now. It was difficult to imagine what he'd given to get to that point. What would he be thinking, looking back across the Channel at that young paratrooper on the other side?
Well now my life is all about closing that loop. It's about standing in France looking across the Channel at the White Cliffs of Dover. Maybe I'll be able to spot that young man so eager to prove himself, prove that he could hold his own and go the distance. Prove it to himself more than anyone else...
One day I will stand on the coast of France, closing the loop and you will be there with me."

PRESS TRIPS

Press trips, also known in the USA as "fam (short for familiarization), trips" are wonderful.

You get everything paid for, are usually upgraded and given lounge access, are taken direct from the plane to the hotel etc.

There can be some long days, but you're taken past queues and lines at events, museums, etc, restaurants lay on special meals, you get to meet the Ambassadors or top representatives of the area you're staying in - and generally have a really good time

Do's:

Do make sure PR firms, tourism offices and other travel industry people that represent places you cover know of your existence and your outlets. This can be accomplished in a variety of ways such as introducing yourself in an email, by mentioning them on Twitter or befriending them on Facebook.

Do RSVP. The minute a press invitation comes in, check your availability and respond as soon as you can. All too often people delay and end up responding too late. A lot opportunity!

Do carry business cards. It's very simple. You want people to know how to reach you. Keep it professional - scribbling your information on a napkin is a no-no.

Do make a point of meeting the host wherever you go. Sounds really elementary, but many members of the media simply skip this critical step.

Presumably, one of the reasons you're at the event is to make contacts.

Don't miss the opportunity.

Do take notes. While most information presented at a press event or on trips can be found "in the release" or "on the flash drive," jotting down notes can help jog your memory. Also, it sends a message to the organizer that you're engaged in what's happening.

Do follow up. When you do write a story that's a direct result of a press conference or trip, be sure to let the organizers of the trip know about it. While you can do this via mentions on Twitter, it's really best to let them know direct via e-mail. Cultivate the personal relationship.

Don'ts:

Don't be a no-show to press events. That will surely fast-track you to the black list. Even if you have to cancel at the last hour, it's better to shoot the organizer an e-mail letting them know you cannot make it.

Don't huddle in cliques. While you may love talking shop with colleagues and visiting with old co-workers, it's rude to other people and often leaves the host and others who are paying for the event standing around on their own.

Don't text or talk on the phone when at events. In fact, don't even take your mobile device out. It's rude and - though widely practiced – is unacceptable behavior under any circumstances.

Don't take pictures of everything you eat. The trend of showing what you ate and posting it on social media outlets, which is suddenly so popular these days, is best left to those amateurs who are tickled to be eating in certain restaurants or eager to let everyone know they are flying off somewhere exotic.

Don't perpetuate the starving writer syndrome. While you may think your laid-back style of dressing is reflective of your creative genius, it's not appropriate to show up at a 4- or 5-star hotel dressed as if you're a street musician.

Don't blabber on about your personal life to the PR folks and hosts of the events. While a certain amount of small talk and exchanging of niceties is in order when meeting people at media events, no one needs to know that your boyfriend of three years just cheated on you or that you haven't made more than $5000 this month.

Don't skip events on the itinerary because you have to work on another article. We all have deadlines. Before accepting an invitation, make sure you're free and clear to go.

Don't take a trip and not write about it.

We've all been victims of assignments that fell through. Magazines close, editors get fired, editors take stories in "different directions." That doesn't excuse you from writing about the destination or hotel you visited. Look for other outlets and opportunities.

Resell, recycle, syndicate...get as much ink, bits and pixels as you can out of a trip.

Make the PR firm that sent you to their client proud.

Keep in mind that someone is investing in you and your reach.

Behind every press trip is a business or a destination that is trying to encourage visitors.

While you may view it as an island escape in the middle of winter, your hosts have expectations. Don't forget that.

OBTAINING FREE TRAVEL / FREE STAYS / PRESS TRIPS

You just need to contact the people in this book, once you've found the resort, tour, hotel, press trip etc that you want to go on.

Give them your name and contact details and where your story or pictures will hopefully appear.

If the trip is abroad, supply your passport details as they will need these for your air tickets.

For press trips, you'll get a full itinerary about a week before you leave.

If you're visiting an area / country independently, they will always arrange hotels, meals, tours, visits, entries to museums etc for you – just say what you'd like to see – or ask them to make suggestions.

ABOUT SELLING YOUR PHOTOS

In order to increase your chances of selling an image, it's important to know the differences between stock, editorial, and fine art images.

And, at the same time, it's important to know that many images will sell well to more than one market.

Although "stock" images technically include all images that are NOT photographed for a specific client or use (that is, photos you haven't been commissioned to create), the term "stock" is commonly used to describe images that are in the collections of stock photography agencies.

These images are often purchased from stock photo houses by a variety of clients - from companies looking to create new ad campaigns or websites ... to state tourism departments for use in a vacation guide ... to magazines and newspapers looking to illustrate an article... to high-school students looking for images to illustrate a book report.

Because competition among agencies is stiff, stock houses often accept only images that are technically perfect and require that photographers provide the appropriate model (and where necessary) property releases.

And, because images need to be technically perfect, it's often the photographers with more expensive equipment that make the most money.

Their images can be sold in larger formats (which cost more and therefore bring in higher commissions) and higher-end cameras often do a better job at creating technically perfect images in low light and extreme lighting conditions.

Editorial images, on the other hand, are the kind you submit together with a travel article or magazine story idea.

They're used to help illustrate a story.

And, they're typically reviewed as one piece of the whole.

As a result, they don't typically need to tell a story independently.

They can be combined to tell a story and they're usually accompanied by a caption of what they depict.

Most camera types (from cellphones to SLR models) are able to produce the type and size of digital files required by magazines (8x12 TIFFs @ 300 dpi is a common request).

And, releases are not usually required.

Editorial images are in this sense easier to license, since releases are often difficult to obtain.

Of the different types of photographs I license, the best-selling for me is the editorial type.

Here are a few tips to help you increase your sales of these images:

Shoot locally:

Let's face it, everyone photographs icons, and you should, too, because they sell.

The trick is to photograph icons in unique or different ways.

Living close to a particular icon will give you an advantage most other photographers don't have.

I have an image of the Statue of Liberty, under heavy snow, which I have sold many times to magazines and tourism publications.

After a huge snowstorm, I snow-shoed to the perfect overlook and took a variety of images in unique (snowy) conditions.

"Shoot with a shotgun first, a rifle later". Especially when starting out, your image collection will need, well, everything.

Remember that icon near your house?

Photograph it vertically, horizontally, at an angle, with people, without people, in winter, in summer, its details, you name it.

Make sure you take these pictures in nice light and that your compositions are strong.

Repeat with the next subject.

Let local publications know you exist.

Once you have enough images of area subjects, send a selection of 20 images or so to the local magazines, state tourism department, and other local publications that might have a need for tourism-related images.

Let them know that you are a local photographer with fresh images and that you would appreciate being on their photographers' mailing list.

Once you get on a handful of these lists, you will be on your way to licensing your images.

Keep Shooting: Things change.

The picture you have of the local shopping scene with everyone wearing bell-bottoms and long hair is now an "historic" photograph (and you should keep it for later).

Keep your collection fresh by re-photographing the same or similar subjects on a regular basis.

WHERE TO MAKE GOOD MONEY

AFAR

Format: Print

Website: http://www.afar.com

Although AFAR does have a website, all of its content appears in its magazine, which is published six times a year.

AFAR emphasizes "real," "authentic" travel.

Think "discover" and "understand", rather than "escape" and "relax."

Types of pieces published vary considerably, from short, destination or service-based lists in the front of book departments, to first person narrative features in the middle of the book.

Do not pitch Spin the Globe, Where Travel Takes Me, Curious Planet, or Good Trips, as those are handled or assigned in-house.

As with any publication, you should read the magazine to familiarize yourself with the departments and style of AFAR prior to pitching.

Submission guidelines: Email pitches to info@afar.com

Pay: starts at $1/word

Editor: Varies by department; consult magazine masthead for information

Contact: As above

American Way

Format: Print and online

Website: http://www.americanwaymag.com/

American Way is the in-flight magazine of American Airlines. Unlike most other in-flight magazines, it's published quite frequently: twice a month.

Most of the print content transfers to the online platform, so there are limited opportunities to publish online.

Editors are looking for pieces from established writers and insist that queries demonstrate knowledge of the magazine and whether a topic has been covered in a previous issue.

Submission guidelines: http://www.americanwaymag.com/AW/ContactUs.aspx

Pay: $1/word

Editors: Adam Pitluk

Contact: editor@americanwaymag.com
Backpacker

Format: Print and online

Website: http://www.backpacker.com/

The purpose of this magazine is to provide both service/destination information and inspiring stories to readers who enjoy the outdoors (and backpacking in particular).

The primary geographical focus is North America.

Submission guidelines:
http://www.backpacker.com/guidelines/

Pay: 60 cents - $1+/word

Editor: Varies by department; see contacts below
Contact: Features & People: Dennis Lewon, Deputy Editor, dlewon-at-backpacker.com

Destinations: Shannon Davis,Senior Editor, sdavis-at-backpacker.com

Skills: Kristin Bjornsen, Associate Editor, kbjornsen-at-aimmedia.com

Gear: Kristin Hostetter, Gear Editor, khostetter1-at-gmail.com

BETA Magazine

Format: Print

Website: http://matadornetwork.com/betamag/

This print-on-demand magazine is the print platform of MatadorNetwork; however, all content in BETA is original to the print magazine.

No service pieces, just straight-up non-fiction narrative that somehow involves or considers motion, journey, and/or place.

Be sure to check the editorial calendar for each issue's themes.

The magazine is distributed quarterly.

Submission guidelines:

http://matadornetwork.com/betamag/writers-guidelines/

Pay: 50 cents/word

Editor: David Page

Contact: editorial@betamag.net

Bike

Format: Print and online

Website: http://www.bikemag.com/

A magazine about mountain biking with a "destinations" department.

Submission guidelines:

http://www.bikemag.com/contact/

Pay: Varies

Editor: Brice Minnigh

Contact: bikemag@sorc.com

Budget Travel

Format: Print and online

Website: http://budgettravel.com/

Budget Travel is, obviously, a magazine targeting the budget traveler; however, pitches should not scream, well, "budget travel."

The magazine is heavy on service and destination features, as well as lists and sidebars.

Submission guidelines: Send a copy of published work as a sample, your pitch (not a completed article) and a cover letter to Submissions, Budget Travel, 530 Seventh Ave., 2nd Fl.,

New York, NY 10018; or e-mail it to Letters@BudgetTravel.com

Pay: $1/word

Managing Editor: Varies by department

Contact: Letters@BudgetTravel.com

Canoe and Kayak

Format: Print and online

Website: http://www.canoekayak.com/

A magazine about canoeing and kayaking.

Pay: Varies

Editor: Editorial team

Contact: letters@canoekayak.com

Climbing Magazine

Format: Print and online

Website: http://climbing.com/

This magazine about climbing is very open to working with writers with limited publication credits, but strong subject knowledge is a must.

Submission guidelines:

http://www.climbing.com/contribute/contributewrite/

Pay: Varies

Editor: Editorial team

Contact: contribute@climbing.com

COLORS

Format: Print and online
Website: http://www.colorsmagazine.com/
COLORS is definitely not a travel magazine, but it is wholly a place-based magazine.

In fact, its tagline is "the magazine about the rest of the world."

Each issue is based around a specific theme, such as money, dance, superheroes, etc.
Recently, the magazine proposed an innovative new way of accepting submissions. See below for details.

Submission guidelines: Writers, musicians, filmmakers, photographers, and artists are invited to upload submissions consistent with upcoming themes to the COLORS website. Editors review every submission and select what they deem the best for inclusion in the printed edition and the online edition.

Upload material here:
http://lab.colorsmagazine.com/about

Pay: Varies
Editor: Jonah Goodman

Contact: Submit material as per submission guidelines above

Edible

Format: Print and online

Website: http://www.ediblecommunities.com/content/

Edible is a collection of food magazines that are specific to cities across the US and Canada; as of this writing, there are 60 different local Edible magazines.

The focus of every Edible magazine is on local food, so every article has a definite grounding in a particular place.

Submission guidelines: Submission guidelines vary by city, so check the website of the city you want to pitch:
http://www.ediblecommunities.com/content/edible-publications/

Pay: Varies

Editor: Varies by city

Contact: As above; check the site for the city you want to pitch

Elite Traveler

Format: Print and online

Website: http://www.elitetraveler.com/

A magazine for, well, elite travelers.
Pitch upscale destinations/ideas.

Submission guidelines:

Email pitches/queries to editor listed below

Pay: Varies

Editor: Mike Espindle, managing editor

Contact: mike.espindle@elitetraveler.com

enRoute

Format: Print

Website: http://enroute.aircanada.com/

Air Canada's in-flight magazine.

Not solely about destinations, however, so read guidelines carefully.

Submission guidelines:

http://enroute.aircanada.com/en/articles/ writers-guidelines/

Pay: Varies

Editor: Editorial team

Contact: info@enroutemag.net

The Expeditioner

Format: Online

Website: http://www.theexpeditioner.com/

TheExpeditioner.com is an online travel magazine based in Brooklyn, New York, featuring travel articles and video for the young and avid traveler.

Articles are often first-person narratives and the goal is to inform and inspire other future travelers.

The publication is open to writers with limited or no previous publication credits.

Submission guidelines:

http://www.theexpeditioner.com/submissions

Pay: Commensurate with experience

Editor: Matthew Stabile

Contact: matt.stabile@TheExpeditioner.com

Geographical

Format: Print and online

Website: http://www.geographical.co.uk/ Home/index.html

The magazine of the UK's Royal Geographical Society, Geographical is much like the US' National Geographic, covering stories that fit within the subject areas of "culture, wildlife, exploration and adventure."

Submission guidelines:

http://www.geographical.co.uk/Home/ About_us/Contributors.html

http://www.travelthruhistory.com/html/ submissions.html

Pay: Varies

Editor: Editorial team

Contact: proposals@geographical.co.uk

get lost!

Format: Print and online Website: http://www.getlostmag.com/

Australia-based get lost! is a travel magazine that aims to inspire travelers "to explore the world and take incredible holidays that won't be found in tourist brochures and advertorial driven publications."

Submission guidelines:

http://www.getlostmag.com/uploads/About/guidelines/

M5437_GL_Guidelines2010.pdf

Pay: Varies

Editor: Luke Wright

Contact: submissions@getlostmag.com

BETA Magazine(online)

http://www.matadornetwork.com/betamag

The flagship publication of the award-winning Matador Network, BETA is the coming together of all that's essential and real about travel - place, motion, gravity, surprise, people, culture, risk, humor, sensory overload.

Submission Guidelines:

http://matadornetwork.com/betamag/art/

Pay: Negotiable

Editor: David Page, Editor-in-chief

Contact: images@betamag.net

Wanderlust

http://www.wanderlust.co.uk/

Wanderlust is the UK's largest and most popular travel magazine and photographers have a 1 in 800 chance of getting published in this highly competitive magazine.

Adding this magazine to your byline is worth the work.

Submission Guidelines:

http://www.wanderlust.co.uk/article.php?page_id=2036

Pay: Negotiable

Editor: Graham Berridge, Art Director

Contact: info@wanderlust.co.uk

Unearthing Asia

http://unearthingasia.com/

Our simple mission is to unveil genuine faces of Asia, presenting quality writings and information that you can rely on.

We touch on the various ways of life unique to each country, uncovering interesting facts unknown to many, and open doors to fascinating sights.

Submission Guidelines:
http://unearthingasia.com/contributors-and-friends/

Pay: $5-30 per photo

Editor: Nikolas Tjhin

Contact: nik@unearthingasia.com

SUN Magazine

http://www.thesunmagazine.org

"The Sun is an independent, ad-free monthly magazine that for more than thirty years has used words and photographs to invoke the splendor and heartache of being human."

This is one of a few magazines which pays top dollar for photographs without sending photographers on assignments.

Submission Guidelines:

http://www.thesunmagazine.org/about/ submission_guidelines/photography

Pay: $100-$300 in magazine, $500 for cover photo, $500-$1000 for photo essays

Editor: Robert Graham, Art Director

Contact: 107 N. Roberson St., Chapel Hill, NC 27516

National Geographic Adventure

http://adventure.nationalgeographic.com/

If you're into high adventure, this National Geographic outlet is for you.

"Adventure covers the world of adventure, from exciting travel destinations and outdoor pursuits to accounts of cutting-edge expeditions and profiles of modern-day explorers. Adventure's primary focus is to enable its readers to travel to, experience, and understand the natural world for themselves."

Submission Guidelines:

http://adventure.nationalgeographic.com/2009/01/about/photographers-text

Pay: Negotiable

Editor: Sabine Meyer and Caroline Hirsch

Contact: 104 West 40th Street, 19th Floor, New York, NY 10018.

Outside

http://outside.away.com

"Outside is a monthly national magazine dedicated to covering the people, sports and activities, politics, art, literature, and hardware of the outdoors."

They are open to contributing photographers but your work must be innovative and must "creatively reflect the essence of the magazine."

Submission Guidelines:

http://outside.away.com/system/ guidelines.html

Pay: Negotiable

Editor: Assistant Photo Editor

Contact: Outside magazine, 400 Market St., Santa Fe, New Mexico, 87501

JPG Magazine

http://www.jpgmag.com

The JPG magazine community is a vibrant network of amateur photographers.

Photographs are posted under various "themes" and photographers can also share photo essays online.

Each magazine print edition then compiles and publishes a selection of the best submitted photography.

Submission Guidelines:

http://www.jpgmag.com/about/photos

Pay: $100 upon publication

Editor: http://www.jpgmag.com/about

Contact: http://www.jpgmag.com/

Outdoor Photographer

http://www.outdoorphotographer.com

If you love sweeping landscape travel photography, then Outdoor Photographer is your outlet.

Published 11 times per year, this magazine is geared towards "enthusiasts with a special passion for nature, travel and outdoor sports."

It offers a fresh approach by encouraging photography "as part of a lifestyle associated with outdoor recreation."

Submission Guidelines:
http://www.outdoorphotographer.com/ submissions.html

Pay: Negotiable

Editor:
editor@outdoorphotographer.com (Editorial questions only)

Contact: http:// www.outdoorphotographer.com/

Travel & Leisure

http://www.travelandleisure.com

One of the top travel glossy magazines on the market.

T+L is published monthly and reaches close to 1,000,000 subscribers and buyers.

Keep in mind, Travel & Leisure accepts photography portfolios in book form exclusively.

Its website states "no transparencies, loose prints, nor scans on cd, disk or email."

Submission Guidelines:

http://www.travelandleisure.com/contact/

Pay: Negotiable

Editor: Meghan Lamb

Contact: Travel + Leisure Magazine, Photo Deptartment, 1120 Avenue of the Americas, 10th Floor, New York, NY 10036

Amateur Photographer

This UK-based magazine caters to amateurs, semi-professional photographers, and hobbyists.

The magazine also runs an annual Amateur Photographer of the Year contest and a slew of other competitions.

http://www.amateurphotographer.co.uk/competitions/

Submission Guidelines:

http://www.amateurphotographer.co.uk/

Pay: £50/gallery submission, £50/page

Editor:

amateurphotographer@ipcmedia.com

Contact: Amateur Photographer, Blue Fin Building, 110 Southwark Street, London SE1 0SU

World Hum

http://www.worldhum.com

Known more for publishing powerful narrative travel writing and other travel-related prose, World Hum also publishes photo essays. Its audio and photo slideshows explore travel through the use of photographs, sound bites, and narration.

Budding photographers can break into this online publication by submitting photo essays that not only evoke a sense of place, but show how travel transforms and changes the world around us.

Submission Guidelines:

http://www.worldhum.com/info/submissions/

Pay: $100 and higher

Editors: Jim Benning, Mike Yessis, and Eva Holland

Contact: dispatches@worldhum.com

Matador Trips

http://www.matadortrips.com

Part of the Matador Network, Matador Trips was created to take travelers "straight to the honey holes, off the tourist trail and beyond the pages of the guidebook."

With stunning photo essays such as Papua New Guinea, Boi Bumbá – The Beat of the Amazon and The Most Alien Landscapes on Earth, Matador Trips is always on the lookout for fresh destination and offbeat essays.

http://matadortrips.com/category/photo-essay.

Submission Guidelines:
http://matadornetwork.com/contributors/

Pay: $25

Editors: Hal Amen and Carlo Alcos

Contact:
hal@matadornetwork.com,
carlo@matadornetwork.com

Transitions Abroad

http://www.transitionsabroad.com

Though Transitions Abroad is geared towards 'non-touring' travelers and is a comprehensive resource for people looking to study, work, or live abroad, it is always on the lookout for fresh new travel photography to grace the covers of its Webzines -

http://www.transitionsabroad.com/tazine/index.shtml.

Transitions Abroad prefers portrait photography and "subjects of photos should be seen in the context of their normal lives, not as interesting curiosities for tourists."

Submission Guidelines:

http://www.transitionsabroad.com/information/writers/photo.shtml

Pay: Negotiable

Editors: Gregory Hubbs

Contact: webeditorial@transitionsabroad.com

inTravel Magazine

http://www.intravelmag.com/

inTravel showcases travel photography that highlight a particular country, city, or area under its 'in focus' category. 8-16 photographs are requested for photo essays, and the showcase with the most reader votes gets compensated.

Submission Guidelines:

 http://intravelmag.com/

Pay: $100

Editors: Christina Kay Bolton

Contact:submissions@intravelmag.com

http://www.guest-travel-writers.com/

"Calling all travel writers"

Guest Travel Writers is a site that offers the opportunity for writers to have their work published. We welcome guest posts from seasoned travellers, new writers and the travel industry.

RECOMMENDED TOP HOTELS

These are some of my favorite hotels – and will usually welcome you, freely.

Geejam, Port Antonio, Jamaica

geejamhotel.com

Originally founded by music producer Jon Baker as a recording hideaway, seven-room hotel Geejam combines ultra-modern technology and the laid-back Jamaican vibe; the signature suite incorporates a state-of-the-art recording studio which has played host to the likes of Gwen Stefani, Gorillaz and U2.

Located on six acres of the verdant San San Estate, the property extends from the foothills of the mountains to the Caribbean beachfront. Guests can chill out in the treetop Bushbar or stroll to Geejam's private beach where they can snorkel, swim, kayak and take in some of the most natural reefs on the island.

The Caves, Negril, Jamaica

islandoutpost.com

A luxurious hideaway located close to Negril's stunning seven-mile beachfront and endless azure waters is The Caves, a boutique adults only all-inclusive property belonging Chris Blackwell's Island Outpost collection.

An oceanfront sanctuary set atop the limestone cliffs of Negril, The Caves features 12 exclusive Cliffside accommodations, private cave dining, a cave rum & cigar bar and serene sea view Aveda Amenity Spa.

Water rafts, kayaks and snorkelling equipment is available and guided snorkelling tours allow further exploration of the numerous caves and grottos.

Strawberry Hill, Blue Mountains, Jamaica

islandoutpost.com

Nestled in the Blue Mountains 3,100 feet above sea level boasting sweeping views of the majestic mountains and Caribbean Sea, lies the blissful Jamaican mountain top retreat Strawberry Hill. Set in 50 acres, the newly refurbished boutique resort comprises 12 Georgian-style plantation cottages.

Part of the Island Outpost collection, it has been a favourite Jamaican spot frequented by many musicians, royalty, and A-listers over the years.

The restaurant at Strawberry Hill serves up Jamaican culinary favourites using local and organic produce sourced from the property's own gardens and Blackwell's personal farm, Pantrepant.

Guests can enhance their stay with nature walks, visits of the nearby coffee plantations, go on bird watching trails or enjoy the hotel's Aveda Concept Spa.

Jumby Bay, A Rosewood Resort, Antigua

jumbybayresort.com

Jumby Bay is a private island retreat just two miles off the coast of Antigua; a world-class all-inclusive luxury resort with just 40 guestrooms and suites as well as Villas and Estate Homes available for holiday rental.

As well as unparalleled views and seclusion, Jumby Bay also offers a great spa, three restaurants, unlimited open bar, all meals and afternoon tea, day sails, an oceanfront infinity edge pool, nightly movies, non-motorised watersports, and snorkeling excursions.

Jumby Bay has been noted as one of the best resorts in the Caribbean and caters wonderfully for all ages.

Rosewood Little Dix Bay, BVI

littledixbay.com

Located on Virgin Gorda in the British Virgin Islands, Little Dix Bay is a true haven ideally located for stunning vistas of the region's natural beauty.

Originally founded by Rockefeller, the villas and guest rooms of Little Dix Bay are situated along shaded footpaths amidst lush foliage, a half-mile crescent-shaped beach, and a colourful barrier reef which is a haven for divers.

Little Dix Bay offers guests chance to sail to any one of the six nearby beaches, decadent treatments at the cliff-top Sense Spa and guided diving through the reefs and shipwrecks.

Also on offer are underwater photography courses, wellness retreats and all-day lobster dining.

Mount Hartman Bay Estate, Grenada

bespokehotels.com/mounthartmanbay

Luxurious Caribbean boutique retreat Mount Hartman Bay Estate is an exclusive eight suite Grenadian hideaway set on its own peninsular with a private beach and hidden in verdant grounds.

The boutique hotel's award-winning unique design looks rather 'Tracy Island' and incorporates a restaurant and all-day bar, infinity pool, Jacuzzi spa, a gym complete with personal trainer on request, and fully stocked library.

The hotel also has its own sea-scooter and superboat for off-shore exploration.

Wining and Dining is a highlight at Mount Hartman Bay Estate with the best cuisine on the island created by Chef Roger, who utilises all the freshest local ingredients to create culinary delights for breakfast, lunch, dinner and snacks in-between.

The Cornwall Hotel Spa & Estate, Tregorrick, South Cornwall

www.thecornwall.com

The Cornwall Hotel Spa & Estate is set in 43 acres of Victorian woodland and parkland yet is just 2 miles from the golden-sanded Porthpean beach, a short drive from the Eden Project and Lost Gardensof Heligan, and the picturesque traditional fishing villages of Mevagissey and Charlestown.

The hotel incorporates a beautifully restored 19th Century manor house, two fantastic restaurants, an award-winning spa, plus 22 two - and three - bedroom self-catered luxury Woodland Homes which enjoy access to all of the hotel amenities.

There are plenty of options for active adventures in the surrounding area including sea kayaking, coasteering and snorkelling; fishing and foraging, cycling paths and walking the South West Coast Trail.

TWITTER

This is a list of the top travel journalists, writers and bloggers on Twitter.

If you follow these, you'll not only get some great ideas of places to visit and stay, but they will often help you with contacts and ideas.

Many work for well-known publications and will be happy to receive your stories and photographs, too!

Finally, by following these in your Twitter account, you'll look very professional, too!

Kevin May – Editor of Tnooz.com (@kevinlukemay)

Benji Lanyado – Travel journalist, Guardian and NY Times (@benjilanyado)

Darren Cronian – Blogger of travel-rants.com (@travelrants)

Catherine Mack – Travel columnist, The Irish Times (@catherinemack)

Carmen Roberts – Travel reporter for BBC World's Fast Track (@carmenlroberts)

Caroline Eden – Occasional travel writer (@edentravels)

Steve Keenan – Online travel editor, Sunday Times (@stevenkeenan)

David Whitley – Freelance travel journalist (@mrdavidwhitley)

Sally Shalam – Guardian and Conde Naste Traveller journalst (@sallyshalam)

Amanda Statham – Travel editor for Cosmopolitan, You & Your Wedding and Cosmopolitan Bride (@Amanda_Statham)

Guillaume Thevenot – Founder of hotel-blogs.com (@HotelBlogs)

Shaney Hudson – Freelance travel writer (@shaneyhudson)

John Honeywell – Captain Greybeard, Daily Mirror (@CaptGreybeard)

Vicky Baker – Journalist specialising in South America – Reuters, Guardian etc. (@vickybaker)

Lisa Minot – Travel Editor at The Sun (@lisaminot)

Francisca Kellett – Digital Travel Editor at Telegraph Media Group (@FranKellett)

Melissa Shales – South African Travel Correspondent for About.com (@melissashales)

Lyn Hughes – Founder of Wanderlust Magazine (@Wanderlust_Lyn)

Jill Starley Grainger – Travel journalist, editor and blogger (@UKtraveleditor)

Annie Bennett – Spain specialist travel writer for UK national press (@anniebennett)

Charles Starmer-Smith – Managing Editor, travel at Telegraph (@Starmers)

Mike Walsh – Travel Weekly chief sub (@mikejwalsh)

Will Hide – Travel writer, The Times (@willhide)

Tom Hall – Travel journalist for Lonely Planet, BBC Radio and Guardian (@tomhalltravel)

Nathan Midgley – Online editor and blogger for Travel Weekly (@twblog)

John Oates – Travel writer (@john_oates)

Mary Novakovich – Travel journalist, The Independent (@mary_novakovich)

Olivia Greenway – Freelance travel writer (@oliviagreenway)

Nigel Thompson – Daily Mirror Travel Editor (@MirrorTravel)

Helen Ochyra – Freelance travel writer (@helenochyra)

Daniel Pearce – Editor of Travel Trade Gazette (@DanielPearce)

Pete Bell – Deputy Travel Editor at The Sun (@TheRealPeteBell)

James Ellis – Travel writer (@worldofjames)

Simon Busch – MSN Travel Editor (@MSNTravelEditor)

Sarah Barrell – Freelance travel writer, Independent on Sunday (@TravelBarrell)

Fiona Kerr – Editor of Conde Nast Brides Honeymoon Guide (@FiTravels)

Paul Revel – Web editor for TTG media (@TravelbizPaul)

Andy Hoskins – Deputy Editor, The Business Travel magazine (@andy_hoskins)

Poorna Shetty – MSN Travel Editor (@MSNTravelPoorna)

Jane Anderson – Author & editor of 101honeymoons.co.uk (@101honeymoons)

Natalie Paris – Travel journalist at the Daily Telegraph (@laParis)

Michel Travel Notes – Founder of TravelNotes.org and writer (@TravelTweet)

Leo Bear – Freelance travel and lifestyle journalist (@leobear)

Lee Hayhurst – Twgroup head of news editor (@leehayhurst)

Michael Kerr – Deputy Travel Editor at the Daily Telegraph (@kerraway)

Kate Simon – Travel Editor, Independent on Sunday (@traveltapper)

Lauretta Wright – Editor of Travel Bulletin (@TravelBulletin)

Sarah Gordon – Journalist writing for TravelMail.co.uk (@SaritaJG)

Meera Dattani – Freelance travel writer for likes of Mail, MSN, National Geographic and Orange Travel (@no_fixed_plans)

Gordon Lethbridge – Independent travel writer (@lethers)
And me of course!

@travel_for_free

MY CONTACTS BOOK – PLACES TO VISIT AND STAY FOR FREE

If a company isn't listed here, don't worry!

Go to Google and search for the company name and press office, e.g.

"(Company) press office"

... and that will take you to the press contact section of the website - and you can often see a link in the footer of their website.

Do be aware, however, that many of the largest companies have separate sites or sub domains for their press pages - this is so that the public don't clog their email and phone lines.

Remember also that my Twitter feed adds 50 – 100 new ideas / contacts / press trips every day.

https://twitter.com/#!/Travel_For_Free

Western Australia

For further information please contact:
Elen Thomas
Tel: 44207 438 4606
Email: ethomas@twa.australia.com

The Southern Spirit, Australia

The Southern Spirit is an exclusive six day/five night rail journey from Adelaide or Melbourne to Brisbane, and vice versa, covering 2,810 kms as it winds its way through four states – South Australia, Victoria, New South Wales and Queensland.

Visit : www.greatsouthernrail.com.au.
Contact : Jovanka Ristich
at jovanka@independent-pr.co.uk.

Amari Ludhiana, India

ONYX Hospitality will run the 127-suite Amari Ludhiana, which will open in the second half of 2012 in the business capital of the Punjab.

Located on Canal Road, a major bypass road in the city, the hotel will be the largest hotel in the Punjab.

Visit www.onyx-hospitality.com.
Contact: Jessica Flood
at jessicaf@hillsbalfour.com.

Nova Scotia

Lindsay Champion

Nova Scotia Department of Economic and Rural Development and Tourism.

P 44 (0)1778 380081

F 44 (0) 870 429 9138

E-Mail nova-scotia.uk@clover-george.com

Direct Line 44 (0)1702-200869

www.novascotia.com

New York State

New York State features 11 beautiful regions with exciting attractions that span from landmarks such as Niagara Falls, and Allegany State Park to family friendly treasures like the Baseball Hall of Fame in Cooperstown and the Museum of Glass in Corning.

Whether it's stimulating outdoor activities, culinary wonders or the rich history and culture of one of the 13 original colonies, New York State offers diverse and dynamic activities and attractions for all travellers.

For more information visit www.iloveny.com

David Gale - PR Manager

Email: dgale@aviacircle.com

Tel: +44 207 644-6121

Fax: +44 207 372-5986

www.nylovesu.co.uk

Red Carnation Hotel Collection

Arnelle Kendall

Vice President of Public Relations

Red Carnation Hotel Collection

110 East Atlantic Avenue Suite 325

Delray Beach, FL 33444

Telephone: (561) 330-0850

Email: akendall@rchmail.com

St Lucia

Windjammer Landing

Labrelotte Bay, Castries. Saint Lucia, W.I.

www.windjammer-landing.com

For more information and mages or to request a press visit to Windjammer Landing contact :

Nina Zapala

nina@anson-stoner.com

407.629.9484 ext. 217

The Finger Lakes Region

The Finger Lakes Region of New York State is the perfect getaway with more than 100 wineries, 11 lakes, charming bed and breakfasts and romantic hotels.

Visitors to the area enjoy the scenic views, extensive culinary scene and the abundance of outdoor recreation offered in and around the lakes.

Visit :
www.visitfingerlakes.com,

Contact :
AJ Shear at aj@visitfingerlakes.com.

Grand Canyon Skywalk

Located at Grand Canyon West's Eagle Point, the Skywalk is the only place where visitors can step out onto a glass walkway nearly 4,000 feet above the floor of the Grand Canyon.

Grand Canyon West is a collection of viewpoints and attractions spread over 9000 acres of the Grand

Canyon's West Rim in Northwest Arizona, 120 miles east of Las Vegas, Nevada.

Visit :
www.hualapaitourism.com.

Contact:
Karen Luard
at kp@kpcommunications.co.uk.

Nova Scotia

Tanya Hillman at tanya.hillman@kbc-pr.com

Shabuway in the San Francisco Bay Area

Shabuway in the San Francisco Bay Area invites food and lifestyle writers to dine at their restaurants in Mountain View and San Jose to experience the traditional Japanese Shabu Shabu (hot pot).

Visit : www.shabuway.com.

Contact Jaslin Yu at jaslinyu@gmail.com.

The German National Tourist Office

For 60 years, the German National Tourist Office has worked in cooperation with the Federal Government to promote tourism to Germany.

Throughout the world it markets the diverse nature of travel to Germany.

It promotes an enormous and appealing product, "Germany as a travel destination".

Visit :
www.germany.travel

Contact :
Nadine Wenn
at nadine.wenn@germany.travel.

Visit Delray Beach, Florida

The Delray Beach Marketing Cooperative wants to introduce travellers to our charming beachside town in Florida.

We are located one hour north of Miami between Ft Lauderdale and Palm Beach.

We stand ready to facilitate your trip by interfacing with local hotels, restaurants and attractions on your behalf.

We'll even throw in a tour of the town via golf cart.

Visit:
www.visitdelraybeach.us

Contact:
Stephanie Immelman
at simmelman@delraybeach.com

Cape Cod, Massachusetts

The Cape Cod CVB markets and promotes the beauty and culture of the resort destination of Cape Cod and the greater region to tour operators, media outlets and meeting planners throughout the world.

Visit:
www.capecodchamber.org

Contact:
Michele Pecoraro
at michele@capecodchamber.org

Premium Land Vacations (St Barts)

Somewhere between being a Tour Operator, a Travel Agency, Vacation Planner and a Concierge and a Lifestyle management company, Premium Island Vacations presents guests with the choice of the best luxury rental villas and deluxe hotels on St Barts, hand picked and selected one by one to provide only the best St Barts has to offer.

Visit:
www.premiumislandvacations.com.

Contact:
James Daltrey
at james@premiumislandvacations.com.

India Mart

India Mart offers Indian trips that include wildlife, leisure, desert, wildlife, beach, heritage, culture, and a adventure tours for all ages

Contact :
www.indiamart.com.

Tariq Shahat
wildlifeandromance@gmail.com

Free Bay Cruises for those visiting San Francisco

If you're coming to San Francisco or if you live in the vicinity, and you're a qualified journalist, Red and White Fleet would like to offer you the gift of up to four comp passes for any one of their bay cruises.

Check it out at

www.redandwhite.com

Then, let me know when you'd like to set sail and we will leave your tickets out for you.

Cheers and happy holidays,

Molly Blaisdell

Hook, Line & Thinker

(mollyb22@gmail.com)

Malaysia

For more information, please contact:
Representation Plus

Flo Powell / Alicia Iglesias Cortes

Email:
flo@representationplus.co.uk
alicia@representationplus.co.uk

Tel: 020 8877 4509/04

Visit: www.tourism.gov.my

For more information on Taiwan, please see www.taiwan.net.tw.

http://eng.taiwan.net.tw/

For media information and images or if you're interested in visiting Taiwan on an individual or group press trip, please contact David Ezra at The Saltmarsh Partnership on 020 7902 1600

or email david@saltmarshpr.co.uk

For more information about Oman please contact:

Oman Ministry of Tourism Representative Office

Sangita Makwana/Alicia Iglesias Cortes

Tel: + 44 208 877 4503/4

Email: oman@representationplus.co.uk

Visit: www.omantourism.gov.om

Rosewood Hotels:

The Carlyle, A Rosewood Hotel - New York, New York
Rosewood Crescent Hotel - Dallas, Texas
Rosewood Mansion on Turtle Creek - Dallas, Texas
The Mansion on Peachtree, A Rosewood Hotel & Residence - Atlanta, GA
Rosewood Inn of the Anasazi - Santa Fe, New Mexico
Rosewood Sand Hill - Menlo Park, California
Rosewood Hotel Georgia - Vancouver, BC, Canada
CordeValle, A Rosewood Resort - San Martin, CA
Al Faisaliah Hotel, A Rosewood Hotel – Riyadh, Saudi Arabia
Rosewood Corniche – Jeddah, Saudi Arabia

For further information on Rosewood Hotels & Resorts visit www.rosewoodhotels.com

http://www.rosewoodhotels.com/en/press_room

Andaz Hotels

Future openings include:

 Andaz Hawaii

 Andaz Austin

 Andaz Costa Rica

 Andaz Sanya Sunny Bay

 Andaz Delhi

 Andaz Turks & Caicos, and

 Andaz Amsterda

Visit : www.andaz.com.

Contact:
Amber Greenwood
at
Amber.Greenwood@luchfordapm.com.

Kempinski Hotel Barbaros Bay Six Senses Spa

The Kempinski Hotel Barbaros Bay Six Senses Spa has been selected amongst the "Best 10 Hotel Spas in Europe, Asia Minor & Russian Federation" by the Readers of Condé Nast Traveller.

Kempinski Hotels, Europe's oldest luxury hotel group has 66 five-star hotels in 29 countries.

Visit:
www.kempinski.com.

Contact :
Gizem Oflazoglu
at gizem.oflazoglu@kempinski.com.

Park Hyatt Ningbo Resort and Spa, China

The Park Hyatt Ningbo Resort and Spa in the eastern coastal city of Ningbo, China has opened.

Ningbo, a prosperous city with a history of foreign trade dating back to the 7th century, is a two and a half hour drive from Shanghai.

Located on the banks of Dong Qian Lake, one of the most scenic areas in the region, the Park Hyatt Ningbo Resort and Spa is surrounded by tea plantations, ancient Buddhist temples, caves and stone carvings, and working fishing villages — a landscape that is reminiscent of a classical Chinese painting.

Visit www.hyatt.com.

Contact:
Emma Powell at
emma@grifcopr.com

The Churchill Hyatt Regency, London

The Churchill is opening its Limited Edition Saatchi Gallery Suite enabling guests will sleep among a collection of Saatchi Gallery works.

Visit : www.hyatt.com.

Contact
Henny Frazer at
henny.frazer@hyatt.com.

Palacio Nazarenas, Peru

Orient-Express will open Palacio Nazarenas, its sixth hotel in Peru, in June 2012.

The hotel is in a former 16th century convent and Senzo, the new restaurant, will only serve carefully prepared locally sourced Andean cuisine, a first for the city.

Visit : www.palacionazarenas.com.

Contact Sara Mirza at

sara.mirza@orient-express.com.

Generator Hostels

European hostel chain, Generator Hostels, has a hostel in Hamburg, Germany - the 6th in its portfolio.

The company has invested 30 million euro in the renovation of the building providing free Wi-Fi in all communal areas, a coffee shop and outdoor terrace and bar.

The 684-bed hostel is located in the Klockmann-House, where the Beatles, recorded nine songs in the 1960s.

Generator Hostels caters for backpackers with hostels located in central Berlin, Copenhagen, Dublin, Hamburg, London and Venice,

Visit:
www.generatorhostels.com.

Contact: Kate Axelby
at generatorhostels@lewispr.com.

Andaz 5th Avenue, New York

Andaz 5th Avenue has added artist Claudia Gold, known as Claw Money, to its art initiative.

The hotel now has four artists; Claw Money, John Hung Ha, Mister Cartoon, and M.Dreeland, and each has painted their "View of New York – Today" on the doors leading to the bar downstairs, located on the Fifth Avenue.

Andaz 5th Avenue faces the iconic New York Public Library and is steps away from Bryant Park in the heart of mid-town.

Visit www.andaz5thavenue.com.
Contact :

Charlotte Hill
at charlotte@grifcopr.com.

The May Fair, London

Situated in the heart of London's Mayfair, the May Fair Hotel was first opened by King George V in 1927 and was once owned by the filmmaking Danziger Brothers.

It has been recognised for having "The Best Hotel Bar in London" by The Evening Standard.

Visit:
www.themayfairhotel.co.uk.

Contact:
Dora Reeves
at Dora@mason-williams.com.

Grand Oasis Palm And Oasis Palm Resorts, Cancun, Mexico

Oasis Hotels & Resorts has reopened the Grand Oasis Palm and Oasis Palm resorts following a refurbishment program.

The new resorts are situated on a protected stretch of beach and have been repositioned as family resorts.

Oasis Hotels & Resorts operates seven properties in Cancun including the Grand Oasis Cancun, Oasis Cancun, Sens Del Mar, Grand Oasis Palm, Oasis Palm, Oasis America, and Sens America.

Visit www.oasishotels.com.

Contact:
Jane Coloccia
at janecoloccia@gmail.com

The Gran Meliá Rome Villa Agrippina

The Gran Meliá Rome Villa Agrippina hotel will open near to the Eternal City during in April 2012.

Located in the centre of the city by the Tiber River, the hotel will be surrounded by shops and monuments such as the Coliseum, Saint Peter's Basilica, the Castel Sant'Angelo, Piazza Navona and the Oratorio del Gonfalone, all within easy walking distance.

Visit :
www.solmelia.com.

Contact :
Anita Keshi at
anita@katchpr.com.

ONYX Hospitality Group operates four diverse yet complementary hotel brands – Saffron, Amari, Shama and Ozo - each catering to the distinctive requirements of today's business and leisure travellers.

The Thailand-based hotel management company also manages a portfolio of independently owned or franchised properties throughout Thailand (www.oamhotels.com).

ONYX reaches beyond its Thai roots to offer innovative management solutions across the Indian Ocean, Arabian Gulf and Asia-Pacific regions.

Visit www.onyx-hospitality.com.

For more information or to request high-resolution photography, please contact:

Jessica Flood

Tel: 020 7367 0941

Email: jessicaf@hillsbalfour.com

Or visit
www.onyx-hospitality.com

Hidden Pousadas Brazil, which offers independent travellers with a one-stop collection of uniquely places to stay, will offer accommodation to travel writers / photographers out of high season.

Visit :

www.hiddenpousadasbrazil.com.

Contact:
Fola Odumosu at
fola@hiddenpousadasbrazil.com.

Norfolk Hideaways, which provides luxury self-catering holiday cottages along the north Norfolk coastline will be pleased to consider press visits to travel writers / photographers with a commission.

Visit :

www.norfolkhideaways.co.uk

Contact :
Kate Morfoot
at kate@junglepr.com.

Newmarket Racecourses offers travel writers / photographers a day at the races, the food and entertainment.

Visit :
www.newmarketracecourses.co.uk.

Contact :
Rachael at Rachael@junglepr.com

Warwick Castle, Warwickshire, UK, invites travel writers / photographers with a partner or friend to get tickets to spend a day at Warwick Castle.

Visit : www.warwick-castle.co.uk.

Contact :
Rosie.Beale@whitetigerpr.com.

Adventure Cat Sailing, San Francisco Bay , will be delighted to 'comp' travel writers / photographers travel writers.

Visit:
www.adventurecat.com.

Contact:
Sharon Schrum
at sharon@adventurecat.com.

BusyBus, Liverpool & Chester, UK, a sightseeing tour operator, will be delighted to host travel writers / photographers and journalists (with a guest) on a review basis. Visit: www.busybus.co.uk .

Contact:
Vera de Ruiter:
vera@busybus.co.uk.

Visit Orlando offers travel writers / photographers visiting on-assignment a complimentary Journalist VIP Passport.

Visit:
www.VisitOrlando.com/media.

Contact:
Amy Rodenbrock
At amy.rodenbrock@visitorlando.com.

La Residencia, Mallorca will be delighted to consider offering accommodation to travel writers / photographers on assignment.

Visit:
www.laresidencia.com.
Contact :
Louise Davis at
louise.davis@laresidencia.com.

The Broadway Collection New York, a group of 17 new and classic Broadway musicals, is always delighted to host travel writers / photographers with a commission.

Visit:
www.broadwaycollection.com

Contact:
Della Tully at
Della.Tully@btinternet.com

Luxe PR, a specialist agency representing 2,000 hotel guestrooms in London and across England will be delighted to host travel writers / photographers for a review stay in one of its central London hotels, or its country house hotels based in Derbyshire, Yorkshire and the Cotswolds.

Visit :
www.luxepr.com.
Contact:
Tamsin Cocks
at tamsin@luxepr.com.

The Mariott Paris Champs-Elysees , which is the only five-star hotel on the Champs-Elysees, will be happy to offer accommodation to travel writers / photographers who are in the city on an assignment.

Visit:
www.parismarriott.com.
Contact:
Bernice Saltzer at bernice@sortedpr.com.

Bath Tourism Plus will host press visits to the Georgian and UNESCO World Heritage city of Bath.

Visit:
www.visitbath.co.uk.
Contact:
Lucy Ryder
at lucy_ryder@bathtourism.co.uk.

City Running Tours of Chicago will be delighted to give free 5k running or walking tours to travel writers / photographers

Visit:
www.cityrunningtours.com/chicago.

Contact :
Marlin Keesler at
marlin@cityrunningtours.com.

The German city of Frankfurt will be delighted to consider hosting travel writers / photographers.

Visit :
www.frankfurt-tourismus.de.

Contact:
Gisela Moser at moser@infofrankfurt.de.

The Cyprus Tourism Organisation will host group and individual trips for travel writers / photographers with a commission.

Visit : www.visitcyprus.com.
Contact:
June Field at
june.field@kallaway.com.

theExplorateur reviews of hotels, shops, restaurants and travel-related products around the world.

Visit :
www.theExplorateur.com.

For press trips to review any of theExplorateur properties, contact
Gabriella Ribeiro Truman
at gabriella@trumarketing.com.

Three Nelson Hotels in Cheshire:

The Grosvenor Pulford Hotel & Spa
(www.grosvenorpulfordhotel.co.uk),

The Pheasant Inn
(www.thepheasantinn.co.uk)

and The Bear's Paw
(www.thebearspaw.co.uk)

will be happy to accommodate travel writers / photographers with a commission.

Contact:
Karen Floyd
at karen.floyd@symmetrypr.com.

Great Hotels of the World, representing over 200 of the world's finest hotels and resorts would be pleased to consider offering press trip accommodation to travel writers / photographers.

Visit
www.ghotw.com.

Contact: Brooke Jester
at bjester@ghotw.com.

The Cranley and The Royal Park two London luxury, boutique townhouse hotels will be pleased to consider providing accommodation to travel writers / photographers on commission.

Visit
www.thecranley.com
or
www.theroyalpark.com

Contact :
Li Boatwright at
li@storringtoncommunications.com.

Mead Brown, a vacation rental company in Costa Rica, is happy to host writers on assignment.

Visit:
meadbrown.com.

Contact:
Michael Brown
at michael@meadbrown.com.

LocalGuiding.com – Personal tours by local guides, will be pleased to offer tours around the world to travel writers / photographers.

Visit:
www.LocalGuiding.com.

Contact:
Robert Blessing at
rb@localguiding.com.

Shakespeare Country, UK, will host travel writers / photographers and their family for one or two nights with passes to visit the attractions and tickets to the Royal Shakespeare Theatre, subject to availability.

Visit:
www.Shakespeare-Country.co.uk.

Contact:
Tanya Aspinal
at tanya@marketingaloud.co.uk.

Mallorca Hotels: Hotel Bon Sol Resort & Spa, Hotel Tres and Hotel Dalt Murada, and Hotel Mar i Vent, Mallorca will be pleased to offer accommodation to travel writers / photographers with a commission.

Visit:
www.hotelbonsol.es,
www.hoteltres.com,
www.daltmurada.com and
www.hotelmarivent.com.

Contact:
Cathryn Hicks
at cathryn@douggoodmanpr.com

Atholl Estates, Perthshire, Scotland will be delighted to host travel writers / photographers. The country estate has historic lodges, modern woodland lodges and a 5-star holiday park. Onsite activities include a pony trekking centre, land rover safaris, stunning gardens/wildlife and the historic Blair Castle.

Visit:

www.atholl-estates.co.uk.

Contact: Lee MacGregor

at lee@leemacgregorpr.com.

The five-star Arlberg Hospiz Hotel and its sister four-star Goldener Berg in St. Christoph am Arlberg, Austria has the 600 year old wine cellar of the Brotherhood of St. Christoph.

Visit :
www.hospiz.com.

Contact:
Karen Luard
at kp@kpcommunications.co.uk

The Villa Pambuffetti in Montefalco, Umbria, Italy will be pleased to offer accommodation to travel writers / photographers.

Visit:
www.villapambuffetti.com.

Contact:
Alessandra Pambuffetti at
info@villapambuffetti.com.

Eustatia Island, British Virgin Islands, an extraordinary 26-acre, low impact, private island estate will be happy to host press visits for travel writers / photographers with an appropriate commission.

Visit :
www.eustatia.com.

Contact:
Alastair Abrehart
alastair@broadswordpr.com.

Africa Safari Holidays will be happy to offer any press trip services to professional travel journalist to East Africa.

Visit:
www.africasafariholidays.net.

Contact:
Agnes Njagi at
info@africasafariholidays.net.

Reykjavik Bike Tours provide press tours of Iceland's capital for travel writers / photographers.
Visit :

www.icelandbike.com.
Contact:
Stefan Helgi Valsson
at valsson@centrum.is.

Champagne-Ardenne Tourisme, four French departments boasting historic sites and chateaux, walking and cycling routes, a variety of sports, superb natural scenery and Champagne will be pleased to consider press visits for travel writers / photographers.

Visit:
www.tourisme-champagneardenne.com.

Contact:
Doug Goodman
at doug@douggoodmanpr.com.

Health retreats on Vancouver Island, British Columbia, Canada.

Visit :
www.vancouverisland.com.

Contact:
Pamela Irving
at livingcomms@telus.net.

Red Mangrove Galapagos Lodges offer a land-based alternative to exploring the Galapagos that until now was a cruise-only destination.

Visit:
www.redmangrove.com.

Contact:
Dave Wiggins
dave@travelnewssource.com

Middlethorpe Hall & Spa , Yorkshire, UK will be delighted to offer DB&B and use of the Spa to travel writers / photographers.

Visit:
www.middlethorpe.com.

Contact: Daisy Parker
at daisy@iscott.co.uk.

Swaziland and Malawi.

Geo Group will be delighted to consider press trips to either Swaziland or Malawi for travel writers / photographers with suitable commissions.

Visit :
www.welcometoswaziland.com

and

www.malawitourism.com.

Contact:
Kelly White
at tourism@geo-group.co.uk.

Holidaylettings, which offers a selection of chalets and apartments around the world will consider arranging accommodation at its listed properties.

Visit:
www.holidaylettings.co.uk

Contact:
Kate Stinchcombe-Gillies
at kate@holidaylettings.co.uk.

Malta will be happy to consider press trips for travel writers / photographers.

Visit:
www.visitmalta.com.

Contact:
Anne Kapranos
at Anne@essence-communications.com.

Peckforton Castle, Cheshire UK, a grade I listed building, built in the 1840s in the style of a
medieval castle will be delighted to host travel writers / photographers on a review basis.

Visit :
www.peckfortoncastle.co.uk.

Contact :
Karen Floyd
at karen.floyd@symmetrypr.com.

Tongabezi Lodge, which is upstream from Victoria Falls, and the new eco-friendly Sindabezi Island are located on the Zambezi River in Zambia.

Tongabezi would be delighted to consider press visits to their properties to travel writers / photographers with a commission.

Visit:
www.tongabezi.com.

Contact
Honour Schram de Jong
at honour@honourway.com.

Ker & Downey Botswana, located in the heart of the Okavango Delta and Moremi Game Reserve, will be pleased to consider press visits to travel writers / photographers with a commission.

Visit :
www.kerdowneybotswana.com.
Contact:
Honour Schram de Jong
at honour@honourway.com.

Adventure Life, which provides small group tours to Central and South America that have a positive impact on the local culture and environment, will consider press trip requests.

Visit :
www.adventure-life.com.

Contact:
Adam York
at adam@sublimepub.com.

Rosen Hotels will be delighted to host travel writers / photographers who will be in the Orlando area, at the new 1500-room, 14-story Rosen Shingle Creek.

Visit www.rosenshinglecreek.com.

Contact:
Mary Deatrick
at mdeatrick@cfl.rr.com.

Migis Lodge on the shores of Maine's Sebago Lake invites travel journalists to experience Maine Lakeside Luxury.

Visit:
www.migis.com.

Contact :
Susan Soltero
at ssoltero@cmcommunications.com.

The North West Development Agency area, which includes Cumbria, Lancashire, Manchester, Liverpool and Cheshire will be delighted to host travel writers / photographers with commissions.

Visit :
www.nwda.co.uk.

Contact : Oliver Bennett
at oliverbennett@blueyonder.co.uk.

The George Hotel, Edinburgh, Scotland, will be delighted to host travel writers / photographers with a commission.

Visit:
www.principal-hayley.com/venues-and-hotels/the-george-hotel.

Contact :
Megan Davidson
at megan@crimsonedge.co.uk.

The Peace and Plenty, Bahamas, will be delighted to provide accommodation to travel writers / photographers.

Visit:
www.peaceandplenty.com.

Contact:
Hazel Heyer
at hazel_heyer@hotmail.com.

The Grand Hyatt San Antonio, Texas, is a 1003-room, 37-storey luxury hotel, which has just opened in the bustling heart of the Alamo City. The Grand Hyatt San Antonio, Texas will be happy to consider providing accommodation to travel writers / photographers.

Visit:
www.hyatt.com.

Contact:
AlisonWood
at Alison@grifcopr.com.

Ranch Rider stays are steeped in tradition, allowing travellers to sample an authentic western experience.

Ranch Rider will be pleased to consider press trip facilities to travel writers / photographers.

Visit:

www.ranchrider.com.

Contact: Siobhan
at siobhan@tionlondon.co.uk.

Lower Zambezi, Zambia:
Sausage Tree Camp located within the heart of the Lower Zambezi National Park in Zambia will be pleased to consider press visits to travel writers / photographers with a commission.

Visit:
www.honourway.com.

Contact :
Honour Schram de Jong at
honour@honourway.com.

Wiltshire, located in the heart of the south-west of England has a number of high quality luxury hotels and a whole host of unique attractions.

Visit :
www.visitwiltshire.co.uk.

Contact:
SamanthaMarsh:
samantha@infinitypublicrelations.co.uk.

Knockomie Hotel, Forres, Scotland, will be delighted to consider press trips from travel writers / photographers for a 2-night stay in one of their 15 individually-themed rooms and dinner on one of the nights in their recently refurbished restaurant, The Grill.

Visit:
www.knockomie.co.uk.

Contact:
Lee MacGregor
at lee@leemacgregorpr.com.

South Lakeland Parks is the north-west UK's leading holiday park operator featuring nine sites within Morecambe Bay, Ribble Valley and the Lake District.

Visit :
www.southlakelandparks.co.uk.

Contact:
Samantha Marsh
samantha@infinitypublicrelations.co.uk

Cumbria Tourism, the tourism body for Cumbria, UK, incorporating the Lake District, will be delighted to let travel writers / photographers sample its delights from the great outdoors and exciting attractions to stylish hotels and high quality restaurants.

Visit :
www.golakes.co.uk.

South Luangwa, Zambia.

The Luangwa Valley has long been regarded as one of Africa's finest wildlife destinations.

Their portfolio includes Kapani Lodge and Kakuli, Luwi, Nsolo and MchenjaCamps. Norman Carr Safaris would be delighted to consider press visits to their properties to travel writers / photographers with a commission.

Visit:
www.honourway.com.

Contact :
Honour Schram de Jong
at honour@honourway.com.

New York Circle Line Sightseeing Cruises will be delighted to host travel writers / photographers with a commission.

Visit:
www.circleline42.com

Contact:
Lisa Chamberlain at
lisa.chamberlain@btinternet.com

The Haweswater Hotel, a new art-deco hotel located next to the secluded Haweswater Reservoir, Cumbria, UK, will be happy to consider offering accommodation to travel writers / photographers.

Visit :
www.haweswaterhotel.com.

Contact:
Samantha Marsh:
samantha@infinitypublicrelations.co.uk

Premier Cottages has a range of stunning four and five star self-catering holiday cottages throughout the UK, Channel Islands and Ireland.

Visit:
www.premiercottages.co.uk.

Contact:

Liz Blakeborough at
liz@blakeborough.com.

St Mary's Hall Hotel, the Isles of Scilly, is happy to provide press trip opportunities to travel writers / photographers.

Visit:
www.stmaryshallhotel.co.uk.

Contact:
Karen Baker at
karen@mercury-pr.co.uk

Woodovis Park, the independently run holiday park on the edge of Dartmoor, Devon UK, invites travel writers / photographers to review.

Visit:
www.woodovis.com.

Contact :
Samantha Kirton at
samantha@independentpr.co.uk

1066 Country comprises the area of Battle, Bexhill, Hastings, Herstmonceux, Pevensey and Rye in East Sussex, UK.

Visit :
www.visit1066ocountry.com.

Contact :
Jane Ellis at
jjmellis@hastings.gov.uk.

The Wineport Lodge, Glasson County Westmeath, Ireland is happy to arrange press travel writers / photographers and can provide a range of story ideas related to food, wine, romance, weddings / honeymoons and spa escapes.

Visit :
www.wineport.ie.

Contact: Nina Zapala at zapala@fzkllc.com.

The Inn on Fifth, a luxurious, 87-room boutique hotel located in the heart of downtown Naples in Southwest Florida will be delighted to consider offering accommodation to travel writers / photographers.

Visit
www.innonfifth.com.

Contact:
Kelly Grass Prieto
at kelly@hayworthcreative.com.

base2stay Liverpool will be delighted to offer accommodation for travel writers / photographers able to review the hotel.

Visit:
www.base2stay.com/

Contact:
Jon Brown at
brown@paversmith.co.uk.

Visit Chester and Cheshire and Visit Lincoln and Lincolnshire will be delighted to host travel writers / photographers with a commission.

Visit:
www.visitchester.com
and
www.lincoln.gov.uk.

Contact:
Oliver Bennett
at oliverbennett@blueyonder.co.uk.

Swiss-Belhotel International, manages hotels, resorts and residences throughout the Asia Pacific, Southeast Asia, China and The Middle East regions.

Visit:
www.swiss-belhotel.com.

Contact:
Ayla Hass at aylahaas@swiss-belhotel.com.

Pembrokeshire, South West Wales will be delighted to consider offering accommodation to travel writers / photographers with a commission.

Visit:
www.pembrokeshire.com.

Contact:
Pat Edgar
PRMatters@dsl.pipex.com

The Rutland Hotel, Edinburgh, will be delighted to invite travel writers / photographers to review this boutique hotel.

Visit www.therutlandhotel.com.

Contact
Yvonne or Fiona
at info@nicheworks.co.uk.

The Galapagos Islands:

Quasar Expeditions would like to invite travel writers / photographers to cover trips aboard the M/Y Grace, its vintage yacht in the Galapagos Islands.

Visit :
www.galapagosexpeditions.com/ gracepresskit.php.

Contact: Paul Schicke
at paul@quasarex.com.

Focus Hotels invite travel writers / photographers to review their three and four-star properties located in key destinations across the UK.

Visit:
www.focushotels.co.uk.

Contact :
Nat Frogley at
nat@bacall.net.

The 5* Blythswood Square Hotel , Glasgow, formerly headquarters to the Royal Scottish Automobile Club, has been redeveloped by the Town House Collection.

Visit:
www.blythswoodsquare.com
 or
www.thetownhousecollection.com.

Contact:
Jo Murphy at
Jo@thespaprcompany.com.

Aspects Holidays specialises in providing self-catering accommodation, from luxury apartments to traditional fisherman's cottages in and around St Ives and the West Cornwall area of the UK.

Aspects will be pleased to consider press visits to travel writers / photographers with a commission.

Visit
www.aspects-holidays.co.uk.

Contact:
Karen Baker
at karen@mercury-pr.co.uk.

The Inn at Lathones, Scotland's only 4 star inn, is delighted to consider press trips from travel writers / photographers.

The 17th century listed building near St Andrews is one of Scotland's oldest coaching inns and boasts 21 recently refurbished external rooms/suites, an award-winning restaurant, an intimate stone-walled bar and converted stables that host regular music events.

For more information visit:
www.theinn.co.uk

Contact:
Lee MacGregor
at lee@leemacgregorpr.com

Cornwall Cottages will be delighted to consider offering accommodation to travel writers / photographers.

Visit:
www.cornwallscottages.co.uk

Contact:
Sue Bradbury
at jess@suebradburypr.com.

Hartland Peninsula Arts, which runs landscape painting courses on the North Devon coast will be pleased to offer courses to travel writers / photographers.

Visit :
www.landscapepaintingholidays.co.uk.

Contact: Karen Outred
at ko@freelancepr.fsnet.co.uk.

Frontier Travel organises tailor-made holidays to Canada in both the Summer

(www.frontiercanada.co.uk)

and the Winter

(www.frontier-ski.co.uk).

The company will consider offering individuals press trips for travel writers / photographers.

Contact:
Dave Ashmore
at dave@frontiertravel.co.uk.

Sail Lofts St Ives, a group of 12 luxury holiday apartments just metres from Porthmeor Beach, will be pleased to consider offering accommodation to travel writers / photographers with a commission.

Visit:
www.thesaillofts.co.uk.

Contact: Peter Hutchinson
at peter@thesaillofts.co.uk.

The Alfajiri Villas and Galdessa Camp would like to invite travel writers / photographers to stay at Alfajiri Villas (www.alfajirivillas.com) or Galdessa Camp (www.galdessa.com).

Visit :
www.FazendinPortfolio.com.

Contact:
Sarah Fazendin
at sarah@fazendinportfolio.com.

The Peat Inn and 5-star restaurant in St.Andrews, Scotland will provide travel writers / photographers able to review the Inn will receive complimentary dinner, bed and breakfast including guest.

Visit :
http://www.thepeatinn.co.uk.

Contact:
Davidson at megan@crimsonedge.co.uk.

The Isles of Scilly will be delighted to consider offering travel and accommodation to travel writers / photographers on assignment, with a commission or who are able to obtain one.

Visit:
www.simplyscilly.co.uk.

Contact: Karen Baker
at karen@mercury-pr.co.uk.

The Park Hyatt Istanbul-Maçka Palas, Turkey will be delighted to consider offering accommodation to travel writers / photographers.

Visit:
www.hyatt.com.

Kathryn Peel at
Kathryn@grifcopr.com.

Helpful Holidays, UK will be delighted to consider offering accommodation to travel writers / photographers.

Visit:
www.helpfulholidays.com.

Contact: Pat Edgar
at PRMatters@dsl.pipex.com.

Jet2.com and Jet2holidays.com will be happy to consider offering flights and holiday opportunities.

Contact:
www.pressoffice@jet2.com.

Wilderness Journeys will be delighted to consider offering press trip facilities to travel writers / photographers.

Visit:
www.wildernessjourneys.com.

Contact:
Stevie Christie at
stevie@wildernessjourneys.com.

Divi Resorts, the Caribbean, will be happy to consider accommodation to travel writers / photographers.

Visit:
www.diviresorts.com.
Contact:
Jacqueline Burton
at jburton@fwv-us.com.

Charming Hotels Madeira will be pleased to consider offering accommodation to travel writers / photographers.

Visit:
www.charminghotelsmadeira.com.

Contact:
Antonio Silva at
asilva@charminghotelsmadeira.com.

Sea Kayak Adventures explore Baja and Canada's newest marine parks and prolific whale watching destinations by sea kayak with Sea Kayak Adventures.

Sea Kayak Adventures will be happy to provide press trip facilities to travel writers / photographers.

Visit:
www.seakayakadventures.com.

Contact:
Nancy Mertz
at info@seakayakadventures.com.

The View Hotel, Monument Valley, Arizona, USA , which opened in September 2008, is situated on the Navajo Tribal Park, on the border of Arizona and Utah.

The View Hotel will be delighted to consider offering accommodation to travel writers / photographers.

Visit:
www.MonumentValleyView.com.

Contact:
Mike Finney
at mike@azcomgroup.com.

The Menzies Welcombe Hotel Spa & Golf Club, Stratford-upon-Avon will be delighted to offer dinner, bed and breakfast at this country house hotel to travel writers / photographers able to review the property.

Visit:
www.menzieshotels.co.uk.

Contact :
Tanya Aspinwall at
tanya@marketingaloud.co.uk

Rosen Hotels will be delighted to host travel writers / photographers who will be in the Orlando area, at the new 1500-room, 14-story Rosen Shingle Creek.

Visit
www.rosenshinglecreek.com.

Contact:
MaryDeatrick at mdeatrick@cfl.rr.com.

The Peace and Plenty, Bahamas, will be delighted to provide accommodation to travel writers / photographers.

Visit:
www.peaceandplenty.com.
Contact:
Hazel Heyer
at hazel_heyer@hotmail.com.

Ranch Rider stays are steeped in tradition, allowing travellers to sample an authentic western experience.

Ranch Rider will be pleased to consider press trip facilities to travel writers / photographers.

Visit:
www.ranchrider.com.
Contact:
Siobhan
at siobhan@tionlondon.co.uk

AIRLINES

SkyTeam.com

Media needing more information:

SkyTeam Corporate Communications
T: +31 (0)20 3333064
E: media@skyteam.com

SkyTeam is a global airline alliance providing customers from member airlines access to an extensive global network with more destinations, more frequencies and more connectivity.

The fifteen members are: Aeroflot, Aeroméxico, Air Europa, Air France, Alitalia, China Airlines, China Eastern, China Southern, Czech Airlines, Delta Air Lines, Kenya Airways, KLM Royal Dutch Airlines, Korean Air, TAROM and Vietnam Airlines.

About Jet Airways

Jet Airways currently operates a fleet of 101 aircraft, which includes 10 Boeing 777-300 ER aircraft, 12 Airbus A330-200 aircraft, 59 next generation Boeing 737-700/800/900 aircraft and 20 modern ATR 72-500 turboprop aircraft.

With an average fleet age of 5.81 years, the airline has one of the youngest aircraft fleets in the world.

Flights to 76 destinations span the length and breadth of India and beyond, including Abu Dhabi, Bahrain, Bangkok, Brussels, Colombo, Dammam, Dhaka, Doha, Dubai, Hong Kong, Jeddah, Johannesburg, Kathmandu, Kuala Lumpur, Kuwait, London (Heathrow), Milan, Muscat, New York (both JFK and Newark), Riyadh, Sharjah, Singapore and Toronto.

About Jet Airways Konnect

Jet Airways' Konnect service operates on key domestic routes, and is designed to meet the needs of the low-fare segment with value-for-money fares. Jet Airways Konnect links seven major metros - Mumbai, Delhi, Chennai, Bengaluru, Hyderabad, Ahmedabad and Kolkata – with several destinations across India, operating approximately 290 flights daily.

About JetLite

JetLite is a subsidiary of Jet Airways India Ltd. and was acquired by Jet Airways in April 2007. Positioned as an all-economy, no-frills airline, JetLite operates a fleet of 19 Boeing 737 series aircrafts. The airline flies to 31 domestic destinations and 1 international destination (Kathmandu), operating 123 flights a day, on average.

Jet Airways, Jet Airways Konnect and JetLite have a combined fleet strength of 120 aircraft and operate over 620 flights daily.

Jet Airways, Jet Airways Konnect, its all-economy, no-frills service, and Jetlite have a combined fleet strength of 120 aircraft and operate over 620 flights daily. For more information visit www.jetairways.com

For further information or images please contact Suzanne Holiday or Lara Jacobs at Keene on
020 7839 2140
or email JetAirways@Keenepa.co.uk.

British Airways

www.britishairways.com.

Contact:
Amanda Allan at
media.relations@ba.com.

Contact the press office on:

Tel: 020 8738 5100

Email: media.relations@ba.com

British Airways Holidays:
Tracy Long
Astral Towers
Crawley
West Sussex
RH11 8PJ
01293 722116

Media in Europe, Africa and Asia-Pacific please
contact the international office at:
Email: international.media@ba.com

Media in North America, please contact the
New York office:

Email: americas.communications@ba.com

Pegasus Airlines

Pegasus Airlines, Turkey's leading low-cost airline, now ranks fifth among Europe's low cost carriers carrying 11.3 million passengers in 2011.

Serving 50 destinations in 23 countries on a Boeing 737-800 fleet with the average age of just 2.51 years, Pegasus expanded its international network during 2011 with new routes into the Balkans, the Baltics and the Middle East.

Visit:
www.flypgs.com.

Contact:
Ceyda S Pekenc
at ceyda@redmintcomms.co.uk

Vietnam Airlines

Vietnam Airlines is the national flag carrier of Vietnam.

Visit:
www.vietnamairlines.com.
Contact:
Nam Bui Hai at
bhnamasia@gmail.com.

KLM

KLM Media Relations is part of the KLM
Corporate Communications department and is
located at the KLM head office in Amstelveen,
the Netherlands.

The department consists of four spokespersons
and a department assistant.

The purpose of KLM Media Relations is to
provide the media with information in a timely
manner and to handle requests for interviews,
recordings and visual materials.

The spokespersons are Ellen van Ginkel, Gedi
Schrijver and Joyce Veekman.

Media representatives can contact Mini Jarvis
and Harriët Veltman, assistant at KLM Media
Relations.

KLM
Corporate Communications
Media Relations (AMS/DR)
PO Box 7700
1117 ZL Schiphol Airport
The Netherlands

Tel.: +31 (0)20 649 45 45
Fax: +31 (0)20 648 80 92
E-mail: mediarelations@klm.com
    American Airlines

Welcome to AA.com's online press guide, your American Airlines and AA.com resource for marketing information, logos and graphics.

Key media contacts and sponsorship requests for technological and marketing inquiries.

Members of the media can direct inquiries regarding AA.com or interview requests to:

Corporate Communications

corp.comm@aa.com

http://aa.mediaroom.com/

Virgin Atlantic

Welcome to the Press Office, Virgin Atlantic's dedicated resource for journalists where you can find all of our latest press releases, facts, figures and images as well as being able to download broadcast and web footage.

http://www.virgin-atlantic.com/en/us/allaboutus/pressoffice/index.jsp

Do subscribe to get the latest news and press trip opportunities

http://www.virgin-atlantic.com/en/us/allaboutus/pressoffice/subscribe/index.jsp

And download their full press kit

http://www.virgin-atlantic.com/en/us/allaboutus/pressoffice/presskit/index.jsp

United Airlines

http://www.unitedcontinentalholdings.com/
index.php?section=media

Star Alliance - 27 Member Airlines

Star Alliance statistics
Member Airlines: 27
Number of aircraft : 4,335
Number of employees: 402,979
Passengers per year: 648.54 million
Sales Revenue (in US$): 158.8 billion
Daily departures: 21,230
Number of airports: 1,185
Number of lounges: over 990
Countries served: 165

http://www.staralliance.com/en/press/

CRUISE COMPANIES

http://www.cruisebaltic.com

Cruise Baltic
Nørregade 7B
DK- 1155 Copenhagen K
Denmark

Jill Faulds
Tel. +44 (0) 1795 89 0100
Mob: +44 (0) 7831 235181
E-mail: jill@jfapr.co.uk

Crystal Cruises

http://www.crystalcruises.com

Welcome to Crystal Cruises' Media Center. Here you will find breaking news, backgrounders, fact sheets, images and a wealth of information about Crystal Cruises and the world's two most celebrated luxury cruise ships, Crystal Symphony and Crystal Serenity.

Media Representatives:
Please contact us for additional information or photography not found here.

Crystal Cruises, Inc.

Media Relations Department

2049 Century Park East, Suite 1400

Los Angeles, CA 90067

Phone: 310-203-4305

Fax: 310-785-3891

Toll Free: 888-799-2437

mediarelations@crystalcruises.com

Carnival Cruise Lines

Carnival Cruise Lines' on-line press room offers the latest news and information on the world's most popular cruise line.

Carnival's fleet currently comprises 23 ships operating voyages ranging from three to 12 days in length to The Bahamas, Caribbean, Mexican Riviera, Alaska, Hawaii, Panama Canal, Canada, New England, and Bermuda. The line currently has one new ship scheduled for delivery May 2012.

Designed as a comprehensive resource for journalists, Carnival's press room includes a "Press Kit and Fact Sheet" section with general information regarding the company and its fleet, along with details on all 23 of the line's "Fun Ships."

Visitors can also read the latest press releases, or visit Carnival's official news blog, "News From Carnival Cruise Lines," which features everything from press announcements to informal posts on a variety of happenings throughout the company.

Travel Writers Contact Page:

http://carnivalpressroom.wordpress.com/press-kits-fact-sheets/

For media inquiries, free travel and editorial photo requests:

Carnival Cruise Lines

Public Relations Department

3655 N.W. 87th Ave

Miami, Fl 33178

(800) 438-6744, ext. 16000

(305) 599-2600, ext. 16000

Fax: (305) 406-8630

E-mail: media@carnival.com

Cruise Baltic

The countries of the Baltic Sea Region have joined forces in order to create a cruise option with fully integrated operations between ports and cities.

The Baltic Sea offers an unseen variety of destinations, sights and adventures for everyone. And with the region's exciting history, rich traditions and spectacular nature, Cruise Baltic invites to a cruise experience out of the ordinary where you can visit 10 countries on a string and experience oceans of adventures.

http://www.cruisebaltic.com/composite-19.htm

Press contact:

Cruise Baltic
Gammel Kongevej 1
DK-1610 Copenhagen V
Denmark

Jill Faulds
Tel. +44 (0) 1795 89 0100
Mob: +44 (0) 7831 235181
E-mail: jill@jfapr.co.uk

Cunard

For over a century and a half, the iconic ships of Cunard have been defining sophisticated ocean travel.

They have always been The Most Famous Ocean Liners in the World.

From fabled vessels of the past to her present royal court — Queen Mary 2, Queen Victoria and Queen Elizabeth — Cunard has carried guests across the great oceans and to the far points of the globe in unparalleled style.

The most glamorous names of yesterday and today have made champagne toasts in her salons, waltzed the night away in her grand ballrooms, savoured grand feasts of the finest flavours in her dining rooms, and whiled away hours immersed in fascinating conversation on her decks.

We invite you to take your place in the rich heritage of ocean travel, and write your own classic adventure tale. Join us for a journey on the legendary luxury ocean liners of Cunard.

http://www.cunard.co.uk/About-Cunard/News-Room/

USA:

The following contact is for media representatives only:
Media Relations Contact:
Jackie Chase, jchase@cunard.com

Requests for digital photography may be sent to Laurel Davis, ldavis@cunard.com.

Log-in information for web access to the Cunard Photo Library will be emailed to you.

UK:

Press Contacts (journalists and media enquiries only please):

Michael Gallagher: 0207 940 5391
michael.gallagher@cunard.co.uk

Eric Flounders: 0207 940 5390
eric.flounders@cunard.co.uk

Gill Haynes: 0238 065 6547
gill.haynes@cunard.co.uk
Out of hours media enquiries:
Michele Andjel: 07730 732072

http://wearecunard.com/

Princess Cruises

http://www.princess.com/news/index.jsp

http://www.princess.com/news/gallery.jsp for free photo's

http://www.princess.com/news/presskit.jsp for full prespacks and info.

Contact

For Princess Cruises UK press office enquiries:

Phone: 44 23 8065 6739

Email: media@princesscruises.co.uk

INTERNATIONAL TOURS

Journeys of Distinction Light

Journeys of Distinction Light, which launches in 2012, will offer trips to Borneo, Burma, Costa Rica, Spain, Italy and Croatia for the budget conscious.

Journeys of Distinction itself is a luxury travel company offering 30 worldwide locations including China, Australia, South America, Africa, Canada, India, Japan, Russia and Sri Lanka.

Visit :
www.jod.uk.com.
For press trip opportunities contact:
Emma at jod@brazenpr.com.

Birding Ecotours

Birding Ecotours provides small group and custom-made birding and wildlife tours worldwide.

We donate a minimum of 10 % of profits to conservation and local communities

Visit : www.birdingecotours.co.za.

For press trip opportunities contact:
Chris Lotz at
info@birdingecotours.co.za.

Discover Walks

Travel Company Discover Walks is dedicated to bringing you fun times discovering major cities.

Join native-born guides on walking tours and authentic, local activities – ethnic cooking classes, photo tours, traditional sports, etc.

Discover Walks launched in Summer 2010. It entertained over 40,000 guests in 2011.

Discover Walks activities are now available in Paris, San Francisco, Barcelona and Prague.

Visit : www.discoverwalks.com.

For press trip opportunities contact:
Alexandre Gourevitch
at alexg@discoverwalks.com.

G Adventures

G Adventures is an adventure-travel company offering affordable small-group tours, safaris and expeditions to more than 100 countries on all seven continents.

The authentic and sustainable approach to small-group travel introduces travellers to the highlights of a destination while offering the freedom to explore it on their own.

Visit:
www.gadventures.com.

For press trip opportunities contact:
Casey Mead
at caseym@gadventures.com.

PlanetWildlife

PlanetWildlife is a leading provider of diverse wildlife travel and tours around the world.

The PlanetWildlife website features over 300 itineraries to Africa, India, and South America, including a range of photography safaris, hiking expeditions and bird-watching trips including ocean cruises to the Arctic and Antarctica.

Visit:
www.PlanetWildlife.com.

For press trip opportunities contact:
Karen Luard
at kp@kpcommunications.co.uk.

G Adventures launches G-Plus

G Adventures has expanded its range of 'comfort' tours with the launch of G-Plus, which offers more than 150 tours in 33 countries.

Led by local 'chief experience officers' the tours include arrival transfers, more meals and trip activities; hand picked accommodation with extra amenities and services and upgraded transport including planes, trains and private vehicles.

G Adventures is an adventure-travel operator offering small-group tours, safaris and expeditions to more than 100 countries.

Visit www.gadventures.com.

For press trip opportunities contact:

Casey Mead at
caseym@gadventures.com.

Greenloons

Sustainable travel company Greenloons has added Alaska and Galapagos cruises and land operators in Sweden and Patagonia to its portfolio.

Visit : www.greenloons.com.

For press trip opportunities contact:
Sara Widness at
sara@widnesspr.com.

TRAVEL SPECIALIST PR AGENCIES

Bennett & Company (USA)

Bennett & Company has spent nearly 30 years as one of the leading public relations agencies in Florida representing hotels, attractions, restaurants, airlines and cruise lines.

Visit:
www.bennettandco.com
to see the current client list.

For press trip opportunities contact:
Laura Bennett at laura@bennettandco.com.

Inaossen (UK)

With the business motto "Quality is not an act, it is a habit", INAOSSIEN works side by side with hoteliers, destinations and other hospitality related companies assisting them to NOT let the emphasis of hospitality lie just in bed and board ... but to make the overall experience of their guests memorable and inviting!

Visit:
www.i-inaossien.com
to see the current client list.

For press trip opportunities contact:
Eleni Koi at services@i-inaossien.com.

Kate Selley Public Relations (UK)

Kate Selley Public Relations is a boutique travel PR consultancy offering a bespoke service to both clients and the media.

Whether you're a travel brand with something to shout about or a journalist looking for original and exclusive story ideas Kate Selley Public Relations delivers outstanding results."

Visit:
www.kateselleypr.co.uk
to see the current client list.

For press trip opportunities contact:
Kate Selley at kate@kateselleypr.co.uk.

Lemongrass Marketing (UK)

Lemongrass Marketing is a fully integrated travel PR, Sales and Representation consultancy.

We help travel brands worldwide to launch, re-launch or re-position themselves in the UK and Irish markets.

Visit:
www.lemongrassmarketing.com
to see the current client list.

For press trip opportunities contact:
Jessica Dollard at
jessica@lemongrassmarketing.com.

Rain Communications

Rain Communications is an independent agency that specialises in news, features and content generation.

We deliver innovative and compelling story angles and packages that cut across print, online, social and broadcast media.

Our core aim is to deliver maximum exposure for our clients, raise their profiles and establish them as leaders in their respective sectors.

Visit :
www.raincommunications.co.uk
to see the current client list.

For press trip opportunities contact:
Alison Wood at
alison.wood@raincommunications.co.uk.

The Global Sustainable Tourism Council

The Global Sustainable Tourism Council is a global initiative dedicated to promoting sustainable tourism efforts around the world.

The organisation works to expand understanding of and access to sustainable tourism practices; helps identify and generate markets for sustainable tourism; educates about and advocates for a set of universal principles.

Amadeus, Melia, Royal Caribbean Cruises Ltd, Sabre Holdings and TUI Travel are among the first group to be recognised by GSTC as publicly committing to promoting sustainable tourism products and services.

Visit : www.gstcouncil.org.

For press trip opportunities contact:
Erika Harms at Eharms@unfoundation.org.

UK National Forest

Media contacts: For further information contact Carol Rowntree Jones, Media Relations Officer at the National Forest Company, on 01283 551211
or email
crowntreejones@nationalforest.org

For background information please visit www.nationalforest.org

Digital images available, contact: media@nationalforest.org

VIRGIN LIMITED EDITION

Virgin Limited Edition is an award-winning collection of unique retreats, chosen for their beautiful locations and magnificent surroundings; each offers a sense of fun, style, luxury and exceptional personal service.

The group includes Necker Island in the Caribbean's British Virgin Islands, Ulusaba Private Game Reserve in South Africa, The Roof Gardens and Babylon Restaurant in London; Kasbah Tamadot in Morocco, The Lodge in Verbier, Necker Belle, a 105 foot luxury catamaran and Necker Nymph, a three man aero submarine.

Virgin Limited Edition aims to make a credible contribution towards creating a sustainable economy and to meet or exceed the expectations of our customers and stakeholders.

Visit www.virginlimitededition.com for more details.

For press trip opportunities contact:

Charlotte Tidball
charlotte.tidball@virginlimitededition.com

Tel: +44 (0)20 8600 0468

COUNTRIES / REGIONS / LOCAL ATTRACTIONS

Germany Hotels

Would You Like To Take A Trip To Germany In 2012?

Maritim Hotels is inviting journalists to enjoy a press trip to one of their stunning German destinations.

With a range of locations as diverse as picturesque countryside to stunning city centre destinations, where will you take a trip to in 2012?

Choose a city break to buzzing Berlin or stunning Stuttgart or experience must-visit events like Oktoberfest in Munich or the Cologne Carnival.

If you can guarantee a travel review and an inclusion of Maritim Hotels in the fact box, what are you waiting for?

Contact us to discuss your visit to Maritim Hotels in Germany (subject to availability).

For further information please contact Rosie Hegarty at rosie@mere.co.uk or call 0161 929 8700.

Visit www.maritim.com for more details on their hotels worldwide.

Italy, Puglia

Please email Concezio
at +353879170517 or email
info@discoverypuglia.com

UK York

Jo Willis at Purebrand on behalf of Visit York
on (44)(0)7896 135205
email: jo@thinkpurebrand.com

Kay Hyde PR Manager – Visit York,
on 01904 554451,
Fax: 01904 554460, email:kh@visityork.org,
website www.visityork.org

Croatia

Croatia; the Mediterranean as it once was, offers 1,244 islands strung along its stunning Adriatic coast, boasts 16 UNESCO Heritage Sites and eight national parks as well as an excellent tourism infrastructure.

From the café culture of its historic cities to the rugged landscapes of continental Croatia, with a packed calendar of festivals and events and a host of home-grown gastronomic delights, Croatia is the ideal holiday destination.

For more information visit
www.croatia.hr
or call on (0)20 8563 7979
Hannah Stalder | Account Manager, Rooster

www.rooster.co.uk

tel +44 (0)20 7953 8778
fax +44 (0)20 7953 8780

email hannah.stalder@rooster.co.uk

EDEN project

- Eden Project Limited is owned by the Eden Trust, which is a fully registered UK Charity (No. 1093070).

-

- Since fully opening in March 2001, nearly 14 million people have visited Eden and it has generated £1.1 billion for the local economy.

-

- So far capital funding of £141.4 million to develop Eden has been raised from a combination of £55.5 million from the Millennium Commission Lottery Fund, £25 million from the South West Regional Development Agency, £26 million from European funds, £1 million from local and regional government (outside the RDA) and £33.9 million in the form of loans, lease finance and Eden's own revenue generation.

-

- Immediate information may be obtained from our website: www.edenproject.com.

For more information, please contact:
Angelina Lambourn
Media Relations Manager
alambourn@edenproject.com
(44)(0)1726 811941
International press trips to Birmingham, UK

The city of Birmingham is looking to work with to generate awareness of the city as a UK weekend break.

Birmingham has been named as one of the top 20 places to visit in 2012 by the New York Times. Alliance members who write for an international outlet in Europe or the USA and would like to be considered for a media visit.

Those visiting the city will enjoy Birmingham for a weekend of fine dining, arts, performance and relaxation stay at Staying Cool, the city's 5* apartments in the Rotunda, an iconic building with panoramic views, enjoy the newly opened rooftop champagne bar at the Cube, visit the Jewellery Quarter, which produces more jewellery than anywhere else in Britain, dine at some of the city's top Michelin-starred restaurants, the city with more Michelin stars than any other English regional city, and take a short trip away from historic centres of Stratford upon Avon, Kenilworth and Warwick

Visit:
www.visitbirmingham.com.
Contact:
Rebecca Cleaver|
at rebeccac@hillsbalfour.com.

Augill Castle, Cumbria UK

Augill Castle in Cumbria is a luxury castle with offering chic bed and breakfast accommodation near Kirkby Stephen in Cumbria.

Augill Castle will be happy to host press visits.

Visit:
www.stayinacastle.com ,
www.golakes.co.uk
and
www.cumbriatourism.org.

Contact:
Rachel Bell
at rbell@cumbriatourism.org.

Press trips to Luxembourg

Visit:
www.luxembourg.co.uk.
Contact:
Serge Moes
at tourism@luxembourg.co.uk

Warwick Castle, Warwickshire, UK

You, with a partner or friend, are invited to get tickets to spend a day at Warwick Castle.

Visit: www.warwick-castle.co.uk.
Contact: Rosie.Beale@whitetigerpr.com.

The DoubleTree by Hilton Newcastle International Airport hotel offers contemporary, upscale accommodation immediately adjacent to Newcastle International Airport.

It has onsite car parking, direct access to the terminals and express links to Newcastle city centre via the nearby Metro line and is a good option for business and leisure travellers seeking a convenient layover, a first port of call in their trip to the North East or to be on time for an early morning flight.

The hotel was opened in December 2011 following a multi-million pound investment by the North-East based Cairn Hotel Group.

Visit: newcastleinternationalairport.doubletree.com.

For a review visit at DoubleTree by Hilton Newcastle Airport contact :
Claire Buchan
at claire@sortedpr.com.

Moevenpick Hotel, Gammarth, Tunis

Moevenpick Hotel Gammarth Tunis a boutique Luxury 5 star hotel and is the unique and modern location.

Located in a exclusive residential area this hotel overlooks the beautiful bays of the Mediterranean and the hills of Sidi Bou Said, the hotel can be easily reached by car from the Airport.

It is only a few minutes away from La Marsa and Carthage, has two restaurants overlooking the sea and a Moroccan restaurant that offers an oriental atmosphere.

Relax in Kallisti spa, which offers a fitness and health club .

Visit:
www.moevenpick-hotels.com.

Contact:
Wissem Arfa
at
hotel.gammarth.sales@moevenpick.com.

Salzburg

Salzburg, birthplace of Wolfgang Amadeus Mozart and location of the immortal movie The sound of Music.

Since 1920 host of the unique Festival "Salzburger Festspiele" and a wonderful combination of great Baroque architecture, modern artwork and the wonderful surroundings as the lake district Salzkammergut or the Saltmines!

Visit:
www.salzburg.info.

Contact:
Gunda Bleckmann
at bleckmann@salzburg.info.

The Oxford Official Guided Walking Tour

The Oxford Official Guided Walking Tour Programme features an extensive programme of themed tours to the city in English and in German, Spanish and French.

New for 2012 are Oxford's Olympic History and the Plaques of Oxford tours.

Visit:
www.visitoxfordandoxfordshire.com.

Contact:
Susi Golding at
sgolding@oxford.gov.uk.

Rabbie's Small Group Tours

Following almost 20 years of success in Scotland, independent small-group tour operator, Rabbie's Small Group Tours, has turned its sights to London by launching its first range of tours departing from the Capital in May 2012.

Rabbie's offers London's visitors the opportunity to explore some of the country's most iconic and spectacular scenery with two to five day tours including Oxford, Snowdonia, Dartmoor, Bath, the Cotswolds, Devon and Cornwall.

Travelling in Mercedes mini-coaches with a maximum of just 16 passengers, the new tours will take guests off the beaten track to experience the real England, its people, history, legends and culture.

Visit :
www.rabbies.com

Contact:
Jonathan Perkins
at Jonathan.Perkins@freshwater-uk.com.

Shark Reef Encounter

Shark Reef Encounter at the SEA LIFE London Aquarium feature a shoal of over twenty of the creatures including two 2.8m long brown sharks and a group of sleek black tip reef sharks.

Visit:
www.visitsealife.com/London.

Contact:
Amy Williams
at amy@freerange.eu.

Tate, London

www.Tate.org.uk.

Contact:
Selina Jones
at pressoffice@tate.org.uk

Alacati, Turkey

The historical town of Alacati on Turkey's Aegean coast with its old Ottoman houses and cobbled streets lined with pavements cafes, and virtually unknown by foreign holidaymakers, is now included in Green Island Holidays' portfolio.

Many of the town's old Ottoman houses have been converted into boutique hotels including the newly opened Beyevi and the Morro, built recently in a style sympathetic to its historical setting in the centre of town.

Others include the converted pasha's palace Nars Ilica; Alacati's first ever boutique hotel, Tas; the larger Solto Alacati and Cadde 75, a modern hotel.

Visit:
www.greenislandholidays.com.

Contact:
Hulya Soylu
at greenisland@redmintcomms.co.uk.

The Chamorro Cultural Theme Park, Guam

Guam is the largest of the Mariana Islands located in the western Pacific Ocean.

Guam's first Chamorro cultural theme park recreates Chamorro life 500 years ago.

Chamorros are Guam's first inhabitants. Lina'la' Park rests on an actual Chamorro village, dating over 1,000 years ago.

Latte stones, pottery, and other artifacts reveal that villagers lived there until the beginning of the Spanish era in the 17th century.

The park features a visitor center displaying cultural artifacts and a brief film about the Chamorro creation belief.

A nature walk filled with tropical flowers, medicinal plants, and fruit trees leads visitors to the recreation of an ancient Chamorro village.

Visit:
www.guampedia.com
and
www.visitguam.com.

Contact:
Jessica Peterson
at jpeterson@visitguam.org.

Meliá Hotels in Mallorca

Meliá Hotels International's comprehensive regeneration project in Magalluf, one of the most popular tourist destinations in Mallorca, will open in June 2012.

The Calvià Beach Resort by Sol Hotels will encompass the Sol Antillas, Sol Barbados, the Royal Beach and Mallorca Beach.

The project will also see the regeneration of the beachfront area.

Visit:
www.solmelia.com/hotels.

Contact:
Anita Keshi
at anita@katchpr.com.

The Manor House Hotel, Moreton-in-Marsh, UK

The Manor House Hotel, Moreton-in-Marsh has won Silver in the Small Hotel of the Year category at the South West Tourism Excellence Awards.

The Manor House Hotel is located in Moreton-in-Marsh, the largest town in the North Cotswolds.

A gateway to the Area of Outstanding Natural Beauty, Moreton provides a great base from which to explore Stratford-upon-Avon, Oxford, the picturesque local towns of Chipping Campden and Stow-on-the-Wold, as well as surrounding villages.

The four-star Manor House Hotel is housed in an historic 16th century building and has just 35 rooms.

Highlights include The Mulberry Restaurant with its two AA Rosettes, The Beagle Bar & Brasserie and the sheltered gardens, where Apple Cottage, a luxurious suite with its own sitting room is located.

The Manor House is run by Cotswold Inns & Hotels, which is an independent collection of properties housed in historic buildings that have been refurbished with contemporary touches.

Visit:
www.cotswold-inns-hotels.co.uk/manor.

Contact:
Sue Heady
at
sue@headycommunications.com.

TOUR OPERATORS

These are the contact details for members of the (UK) Association of Independent Tour Operators, who are all ready and available to help you organize free travel and free stays worldwide.

Look each company up, find a tour that you like and email the person named.
.
All telephone numbers are UK.

For the USA equivalent, please see
http://www.ustoa.com/
onlinekit/USTOAMembers.pdf
for an up to date list.

You also can - and should! – register for their press releases, which contain many offers for their members).

Gina Sisco
Redpoint Marketing PR, Inc.
phone: (212) 229-0119
fax: (212) 229-0364

e-mail: dsisco@redpointpr.com

1st Class Holidays www.1stclassholidays.com
Jonathan Whiteley
jonathan.whiteley@1stclassholidays.com 0845
644 3939

A Golfing Experience
www.agolfingexperience.com
Steven Frewin
steve@agolfingexperience.com
01923 28 33 39

Abercrombie & Kent Travel
www.abercrombiekent.co.uk
Frangelica Flook
fflook@abercrombiekent.co.uk
020 7978 4534

Absolute Escapes
www.absoluteescapes.com
Andy Gabe
info@absoluteescapes.com
0131 4472570

ACE Cultural Tours
www.aceculturaltours.co.uk
Julia Berg
julia@juliabergconsulting.co.uk
07989 353066

Adventure Alternative
www.adventurealternative.com
Gavin Bate
gavin@adventurealternative.com

02890 701476

Africa and Beyond
www.africa-and-beyond.co.uk
Richard Russell
richard@africa-and-beyond.co.uk
0161 789 8838

Africa Collection
www.africacollection.com
Chris Fortescue
chris@africacollection.com
01403 256655

All Ways Pacific
www.all-ways.co.uk
John Rankin   john@all-ways.co.uk
01494 432747

Alpine Action
www.alpineaction.co.uk
Dionne Heasman
dionne@alpineaction.co.uk
01273 466 535

Anatolian Sky Holidays
www.anatoliansky.co.uk
Carole Pugh
carole@fourcornerspr.co.uk
0117 9446617

Andante Travels
www.andantetravels.co.uk
Saffia Bhutta
Safia@andantetravels.co.uk
01722 713800

Arblaster & Clarke Wine Tours
www.winetours.co.uk
Lynette Arblaster
lynette@winetours.co.uk
01730 263 111

Archipelago Azores
www.azoreschoice.com
Ian Coates
ian@azoreschoice.com
017687 75672

Audley Travel
www.audleytravel.com
Jemma Hewlett
jemma.hewlett@btinternet.com
01491 614660

Authentic Adventures
www.authenticadventures.co.uk
 Linda Kember
linda@authenticadventures.co.uk
01453 823328

Baltic Holidays

www.balticholidays.com
Phil Teubler
phil@balticholidays.com
0845 0705711

Beachcomber
www.beachcombertours.co.uk
Mark Boullé
mboulle@bctuk.com
01483 445690

Bents Bicycle & Walking Tours
www.bentstours.com
Stephen Bent
stephen@bentstours.com
01568 780800

Bridge & Wickers
www.bridgeandwickers.co.uk
David Wickers
davidw@bridgeandwickers.com
020 7483 6551

Brightwater Holidays
www.brightwaterholidays.com
Graeme Mitchell
graeme@brightwaterholidays.com
01334 657155

Bushbaby Travel
www.bushbaby.travel
Abi Shaw

abi@bushbaby.travel
01252 792 984

Cachet Travel
www.cachet-travel.co.uk
Thorsten Fibelkorn
thorsten@cachet-travel.co.uk
020 8847 8700

Carrier
www.carrier.co.uk
Natasha Sawney
natasha.sawney@carrier.co.uk
0161 491 7674

Casas Cantabricas
www.casas.co.uk
Andy McCulloch
andy@casas.co.uk
01223 328721

Cedarberg African Travel
www.cedarbergtravel.com
Ginny Russell
ginny@cedarberg-travel.com
020 8898 8533

Ciceroni Travel
www.ciceroni.co.uk
Stephen Brook
stephenbrook@ciceroni.co.uk
01869 811167

Cities Direct
www.citiesdirect.co.uk/aito
Jace Quick
jace@citiesdirect.co.uk
01242 536908

Classic Collection Holidays
www.classic-collection.co.uk
Andrew Farr
andrew.farr@classic-collection.co.uk
01903 836611

Classic Tours
www.classictours.co.uk
Gina Thomas   admin@classictours.co.uk
020 7619 0066

Collette Worldwide Holidays
www.colletteworldwide.com
Steve Stuart
sstuart@colletteworldwide.com
01895203456

Collett's Mountain Holidays
www.colletts.co.uk
Tom Collett
tom@colletts.co.uk
01799513331

Corsican Places

www.corsica.co.uk
Jenny Adams
jenny.adams@serenityholidays.co.uk
01489 866963

Cox & Kings Travel
www.coxandkings.co.uk
Katie Parsons
katie.parsons@coxandkings.co.uk
020 7873 5006

CTS Horizons
www.ctshorizons.com
Heather Chan
h.chan@ctsuk.com
020 7868 5599

Danube Express
www.danube-express.com
Julia Spence
juliaspence.pr@gmail.com
01491 824524

Discover
www.kasbahdutoubkal.com
Mike McHugo
mike@discover.ltd.uk
01883 744392

Discover Adventure
www.discoveradventure.com
Kathryn Furnell

kathryn@discoveradventure.com
01722 719038

Discover the World
www.discover-the-world.co.uk
Georgina Hancock
georgina@discover-the-world.co.uk
01737 214 204

Distinctive Americas
www.distinctiveamericas.com
Daniel Benians
daniel@distinctiveamericas.com
01242 890555

Dragoman
www.dragoman.com
Rebecca Scrase
rebecca@dragoman.co.uk
01449 677033

Equestrian Escapes
www.equestrian-escapes.com
Sarah Caplan
sarahcaplan@equestrian-escapes.com
01829 781123

Eurocamp
www.eurocamp.co.uk
Emma Flinn
e.flinn@amaze.com
0161 838 8716

Experience Travel
www.experiencetravelgroup.com
Sam Clark
sam@experiencetravelgroup.com
020 7924 7133

Expert Africa   www.expertafrica.com
Chris McIntyre
chris.mcintyre@expertafrica.com
020 8232 9777

Explore
www.explore.co.uk
Stella Blackwell
stella.blackwell@explore.co.uk
01252 379 505

Expressions Holidays
www.expressionsholidays.co.uk
Martin Garland
mgarland@expressionsholidays.co.uk
01752 878 099

Ffestiniog Travel
www.ffestiniogtravel.com
Karen Carpenter
k.carpenter@travelpr.co.uk
020 8891 4440

Fleewinter

www.fleewinter.com
Mick Thompson
mick@mediacontactspr.co.uk
0207 112 0019

Frontier Travel
www.frontier-travel.co.uk
Dave Ashmore
dave@frontier-travel.co.uk
020 8776 8709

Geodyssey
www.geodyssey.co.uk
John Thirtle
john@geodyssey.co.uk
020 7281 7788

GIC - The Villa Collection
www.gicvillas.com
Penny Law
p.law@travelpr.co.uk
020 8891 4440

Golf Amigos
www.golfamigos.co.uk
Gordon Murray
Gordon@golfamigos.co.uk
0141 644 0999

Grape Escapes
www.grapesescapes.net
Mark Hallett
mark@grapeescapes.net

01763 273373

Great Escapes
www.greatescapes.co.uk
Jenny Adams
jenny.adams@serenityholidays.co.uk
01489 866963

Great Rail Journeys
www.GreatRail.com
Giles Latham
gileslatham@greatrail.com
01904 521900

Greaves Travel
www.greavesindia.com
Tanya Dalton
tdalton@greavesuk.com
020 7487 9111

Greek Options
www.greekoptions.co.uk
Alan Bates
alan@greekoptions.co.uk
01442 891 972

Heritage Group Travel
www.grouptravel.co.uk
John Iles
jiles@grouptravel.co.uk
01225 466620

High Places
www.highplaces.co.uk
Paul Adams
paul@highplaces.co.uk
0845 257 7500

IBT Travel
www.ibttravel.com
Jennifer Sharpe
jennifers@ibt-travel.com
01292 477771

If Only
www.ifonly.net
Tom Higgins
tomh@ifonly.net
0141 955 4043

In The Saddle
www.inthesaddle.com
James Sales
james@inthesaddle.com
01299 272 232

Indus Tours & Travel
www.industours.co.uk
Yasin Zargar
yasin@industours.co.uk
020 8901 7320

Inntravel
www.inntravel.co.uk

Julia Spence
juliaspence.pr@googlemail.com
01491 824524

Inscape Fine Art Study Tours
www.inscapetours.co.uk
Sara Pupi
sara@inscapetours.co.uk
07701055384

Inside Japan Tours
www.insidejapantours.com
James Mundy
james@insidejapantours.com
0117 3144620

International Travel Connections
www.itcclassics.co.uk
Jane Heywood
janeheywood@itc-uk.com
01244 355400

Ionian Island Holidays
www.ionianislandholidays.com
Bernadette Askouni
bernadette@ionianislandholidays.com
020 8459 0777

Jacada Travel
www.jacadatravel.com
Alex Malcolm
alex@jacadatravel.com

020 7562 8261

Journey Latin America
www.journeylatinamerica.co.uk
Laura Rendell-Dunn
laura.rendell-dunn@journeylatinamerica.co.uk
020 8622 8422

Just Grenada
www.justgrenada.co.uk
Gerry Copsey
gerrycopsey@justgrenada.co.uk
01373 814214

Just Sardinia
www.justsardinia.co.uk
Alison Nurse
alison@justsardinia.co.uk
07818 484747

KE Adventure Travel
www.keadventure.com
Tim Greening
tim@keadventure.com
01768 771701

Kerala Connections
www.keralaconnections.co.uk
Diana Syrett
DianaS@keralaconnections.co.uk
01892 722440

Kirker Holidays
www.kirkerholidays.com
Karen Carpenter
k.carpenter@travelpr.co.uk
020 8891 4440

Kudu Travel
www.kudutravel.com
Fi Lowry
kuduinfo@kudutravel.com
01722 716167

La Joie de Vivre
www.lajoiedevivre.co.uk
Paul Lodge
paul@lajoiedevivre.co.uk
01483 272379

Last Frontiers
www.lastfrontiers.com
Edward Paine
aito@lastfrontiers.com
01296 653000

Limosa Holidays
www.limosaholidays.co.uk
Chris Kightley
chris@limosaholidays.co.uk
01692 580623

Llama Travel
www.llamatravel.com

Luca Newbold
lnewbold@llamatravel.com
020 7281 9689

Long Travel - Southern Italy
www.long-travel.co.uk
Laura Jones
laura@long-travel.co.uk
01694 722193

Macs Adventure
www.macsadventure.com
Neil Lapping
neil@macsadventure.com
0141 255 0103

Martin Randall Travel
www.martinrandall.com
Liz Brown
liz.brown@martinrandall.co.uk
020 8742 3355

McCabe Pilgrimages
www.mccabe-travel.co.uk
Alistair McCabe
alistair@mccabe-travel.co.uk
020 8675 6828

McKinlay Kidd
www.mckinlaykidd.co.uk
Carole Pugh
carole@fourcornerspr.co.uk

0117 9446617

Mickledore Travel
www.mickledore.co.uk
Rick Cooper
rick@mickledore.co.uk
017687 72335

Minorca Sailing Holidays
www.minorcasailing.co.uk
Ian Aldridge
enquiries@minorcasailing.co.uk
020 8948 2106

Mosaic Holidays
www.mosaicholidays.co.uk
Gary Wedekind
sales@mosaicholidays.co.uk
020 8574 4000

Motor Racing International
www.motorracinginternational.uk.com
Gary Howell
gary@motorracinginternational.uk.com
01304 612424

Mountain Kingdoms
www.mountainkingdoms.com
Steve Berry
steve@mountainkingdoms.com
01453 844400

Naturetrek
www.naturetrek.co.uk
David Mills
david@naturetrek.co.uk
01962 733051

Nomadic Thoughts
www.nomadicthoughts.com
Jono Vernon-Powell
Jono@nomadicthoughts.com
020 7604 4408

Oasis Overland
www.oasisoverland.co.uk
Ceris Borthwick
ceris@oasisoverland.co.uk
079 3234 7955

Okavango Tours & Safaris
www.okavango.com
Jane Durham
jane@okavango.com
020 8347 4030

On Foot Holidays
www.onfootholidays.co.uk
Simon Scutt
simon@onfootholidays.co.uk
01722 322652

On the Go Tours
www.onthegotours.com

Pru Goudie
pru@onthegotours.com
020 7471 6413

Original Travel
www.originaltravel.co.uk
Jules Herbert
jules@originaltravel.co.uk
020 7978 7333

Oxalis Holidays
www.oxalis-adventures.com
Matt Malcomson
matt@oxalis-holidays.com
020 7099 6147

Pax Travel
www.paxtravel.co.uk
Andrew Merryweather
andrew.merryweather@paxtravel.co.uk
020 7485 3003

Peter Sommer Travels
www.petersommer.com
Peter Sommer
peter@petersommer.com
01600 888220

Planos Holidays
www.planos.co.uk
Karen Outred
ko@freelancepr.fsnet.co.uk
01189 401893

Prestige Holidays
www.prestigeholidays.co.uk
Liz Blakeborough
liz@blakeborough.com
0117 924 0868

Pure Crete
www.purecrete.com
Louise Kilner
info@purecrete.com
0845 070 1571

Ramblers Worldwide Holidays
www.ramblersholidays.co.uk
Tony Maniscalco
tonym@ramblersholidays.co.uk
01707 386755

Regaldive
www.regaldive.co.uk
Stella Blackwell
Stella.brown@regal-diving.co.uk
01252 379 505

Rhapsody Tours
www.rtours.co.uk
John Baines
sales@rtours.co.uk
01732 750739

Ride World Wide

www.rideworldwide.com
Ruth Taggart
info@rideworldwide.com
01837 82544

Safari Consultants
www.safari-consultants.co.uk
Bill Adams
bill@safariconsultantuk.com
01787 888 590

Safari Drive
www.safaridrive.com
Emma Hanlon
emma@safaridrive.com
01488 71140

Sailing Holidays
www.sailingholidays.com
Patrick Eley
pat@sailingholidays.com
020 8438 1130

Scandinavian Travel
www.scandinavian-travel.co.uk
Oben Murat
ben@ski-norway.co.uk
0047 984 87188

Scott Dunn
www.scottdunn.com
Clair Horwood

Clair.Horwood@scottdunn.com
0208 682 5083

Seasons
www.seasons.co.uk
Jo Clarkson
jo@seasons.co.uk
01244 206 062

Serenity Holidays
www.serenityholidays.co.uk
Jenny Adams
jenny.adams@serenityholidays.co.uk
01489 866 963

Ski Peak
www.skipeak.net
Nigel Purkhardt
nigel@skipeak.com
01428 608070

Ski Safari
www.skisafari.com
Vicky Bamford
vicky@skisafari.com
01273 224060

Ski Weekend
www.skiweekend.com
Gavin Foster
gavin@skiweekend.com
00336 15195427

Snowbizz
www.snowbizz.co.uk
Wendy Lyotier
wendy@snowbizz.co.uk
01778 341 455

Specialised Tours
www.specialisedtours.com
Margaret Scowen
margaret@specialisedtours.com
01342 712785

Sports Tours
www.sportstours.co.uk
Stephen Da Costa
steve@sportstours.co.uk
01708 344001

Sports Travel International
www.stisport.com
Ashley Gowing
ashley@stisport.com
01279 661700

Sunvil Holidays
www.sunvil.co.uk
Anthony Sebastian
a.sebastian@travelpr.co.uk
020 8891 4440

Sunvil Traveller

www.sunvil.co.uk
Lloyd Boutcher
lloyd.boutcher@sunvil.co.uk
020 8232 9789

Tangney Tours
www.tangney-tours.com
Nicholas Tangney
nicholas@tangney-tours.com
01732 886666

The Discovery Collection
www.thediscoverycollection.com
Zekiye Yucel
zy@thediscoverycollection.com
01371 859733

The Russia Experience
www.trans-siberian.co.uk
Odette Fussey
odette@trans-siberian.co.uk
0845 521 2910

The Travelling Naturalist
www.naturalist.co.uk
Jamie McMillan
jamie@naturalist.co.uk
01305 267994

TransIndus
www.transindus.co.uk
Julia Spence

juliaspence.pr@gmail.com
01491 824 524

Travel Destinations
www.traveldestinations.co.uk
Andrew Melley
andrew@traveldestinations.co.uk
01707 329988

Travelux Holidays
www.traveluxgreece.co.uk
Bob Cooper
cooper.rw@gmail.com
01580 765000

Tribes Travel
www.tribes.co.uk
Amanda Marks
amanda@tribes.co.uk
01728 685971

Tropic Breeze
www.tropicbreeze.co.uk
Jo Plummer
jo@tropicbreeze.co.uk
01752880880

Tucan Travel
www.tucantravel.com
Ben McIntosh
ben@tucantravel.com
020 8896 6711

Vacations to America
www.vacationstoamerica.com
Richard Wimms
richard@vacationsgroup.co.uk
01582 469661

Veloso Tours
www.veloso.com
Paulo Veloso
paulo@veloso.com
020 8762 0616

Venue Holidays
www.venueholidays.co.uk
Andrew Burden
andrew@venueholidays.co.uk
01233 629955

VIP & Coastline
www.vip-chalets.com
Nicola Hardy
nicola.hardy@vip-chalets.com
0844 557 3119

Visions Holiday Group
www.visionsholidaygroup.co.uk
Zoe Cornwall
zoe.cornwall@islands-of-greece.co.uk
01444 225626

Voyager World Travel

www.voyagercuba.co.uk
Ian Settle
mail@voyagerworldtravel.co.uk
01580 766222

Wendy Wu Tours
www.wendywutours.co.uk
Jules Ugo
jules@lotus-uk.co.uk
020 7953 7470

Wild Frontiers
www.wildfrontiers.co.uk
Nat Morris
nat@wildfrontiers.co.uk
020 7736 3968

Wildlife Trails
www.wildlifetrails.co.uk
Allan Blanchard
info@wildlifetrails.co.uk
01946 841495

Wilderness Scotland
www.wildernessscotland.com
Julia Spence
juliaspence.pr@gmail.com
01491 824 524

ACKNOWLEDGEMENTS AND THANK YOU

Jack Freemont would like to record his appreciation for all the help and assistance given by the countries, resorts, hotels, cruise companies, tour operators and PR companies in the preparation of this book – far to many names to mention individually ... although many individuals are named throughout the book!

A big thank you to you all.

CPSIA information can be obtained
at www.ICGtesting.com
Printed in the USA
BVHW041353110121
597543BV00006B/241